AFRICA

Vol. 74 No. 1 2004

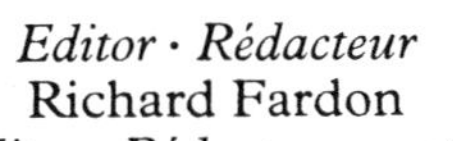

Editor · Rédacteur
Richard Fardon
Reviews Editor · Rédacteur comptes-rendus
Paul Nugent
Consultant Editors · Rédacteurs consultatifs
Thomas J. Bassett · Filip de Boeck · Alcinda Honwana · Deborah James
Murray Last · Tandeka Nkiwane · Mwenda Ntarangwi · Alula Pankhurst

GRANDPARENTS AND GRANDCHILDREN

Guest editors: Wenzel Geissler, Erdmute Alber and Susan Whyte

Journal of the International African Institute
Revue de l'Institut Africain International

LIFETIMES INTERTWINED: AFRICAN GRANDPARENTS AND GRANDCHILDREN

Susan R. Whyte
Erdmute Alber
P. Wenzel Geissler

In this volume we return to one of the treasures of our contributors' anthropological heritage: the study of kinship in Africa. We have chosen to focus on the intertwined lives of grandparents and grandchildren because they raise so clearly fundamental issues of temporality and relationship. While grandparents and grandchildren live together in shared time, their lifetimes overlap only partly. They have different pasts and different futures, and they share a present that in many countries is being radically affected by historical transformations such as urbanisation, impoverishment and the scourge of AIDS.

The collection grew out of a panel presented at the 2002 conference of the Association of Social Anthropologists of the United Kingdom and the Commonwealth (ASA). The theme of that meeting in Arusha, organised by Wendy James and David Mills, was 'Perspectives on Time and Society: Experience, Memory, History'.[1] The ASA itself was founded in 1946 by E. E. Evans-Pritchard, one of the giants in the social anthropology of Africa. He and others like A. R. Radcliffe-Brown, Meyer Fortes and Jack Goody laid out a set of issues concerning kinship, marriage and domestic groups that were well illustrated by the position of grandparents. The articles presented here build on their interests in kinship and generation while opening new perspectives and raising new questions. Three main themes run from the early studies through this recent research.

CATEGORIES AND LIVES

The structure of society in terms of kinship categories based on gender and generation was fundamental to the work of our (British) anthropological ancestors. On the one hand, scholars emphasised the equivalence of alternate generations and the opposition between proximate ones. On the other, they were concerned with lineality and

---

[1] The ASA conference, where this collection began as a panel, received generous financial support from the Ford Foundation and OSSREA (Organisation for Social Science Research in Eastern and Southern Africa) which enabled the participation of almost forty Africa-based scholars. Ethiopia, Eritrea, Sudan, Kenya, Tanzania, South Africa, Zimbabwe, Nigeria and Uganda were all represented among these. A British Academy grant supported the travel of sixteen participants from Britain, and two more were assisted by the Swan Fund at Oxford University. A grant from the RAI (Royal Anthropological Institute) enabled the travel of two of the conference's four key-note speakers. The ASA supported the travel and subsistence of a number of its members and scholars from the region.

the degree of distinction between matrilateral and patrilateral relations. Several of the articles in this collection follow these lines, confirming and also criticising the relevance of such categories. Notermans writing on eastern Cameroon and Alber working in Benin explore systems of fosterage in which grandparents can assume the role of parents, thus blurring the distinction between alternate and proximate generations. Ingstad from Botswana and Whyte and Whyte from eastern Uganda report on the continuing significance of lineality (or laterality) in the sense that the children of sons and of daughters are differently placed in relation to grandparents. Notermans challenges earlier understandings of lineality in Cameroon by showing how grandmothers fostering the children of their daughters in a supposedly patrilineal society try to keep their grandchildren in a matrilineal pattern by identifying a male member of the maternal family as the child's father in the registry offices. For Notermans, grandmothers are the 'main actors' in a parallel matrilineal descent system. Thus, she argues, 'African kinship systems have been misconstrued through neglecting grandmothers' agency in matters of descent.'

Both Notermans and Alber go beyond a categorical view of gender, generation and descent in that they conceptualise kinship as a mode of exchange, in which people can be seen as gifts. In contrast to the often criticised view of men exchanging women in marriage, they show how small children are exchanged, reclaimed and taken by grandmothers. Very explicitly, Alber conceptualises the giving of grandchildren to grandparents as 'part of a complex process of intergenerational exchange that is essential to kinship relations among the Baatombu'. But far from the formalist approach of the 'French' ancestors, which neglected the actor's perspective, the notion of fostered grandchildren as 'gifts' is combined with the recognition of subjectivity and experience. It is noteworthy, however, that the viewpoint is that of the grandparents and not the grandchildren.

Although questions of structure and classification (including the compass of the category 'grandparent') remain relevant, most of the articles here are concerned with people as actors who invoke categories and shape relationships. Notermans is most explicit on this point; inspired by Johnson-Hanks (2002), she argues that women in Batouri navigate a life course in which grandmotherhood is achieved and practised rather than simply undergone at a certain stage of life.

QUALITIES OF RELATIONSHIP

The special quality of relationships to grandparents has long been remarked by anthropologists. In his introduction to *African Systems of Kinship and Marriage*, Radcliffe-Brown (1950) wrote that hierarchy and formality characterise interactions between proximate generations, while the equivalence of alternate ones allows equality and even intimacy. Fortes's description of the contrast among the Tallensi pointed out that conflicts (over property and behaviour) occurred between parents and children. Grandparents were warm and sympathetic; they left discipline and allocation of resources to their grandchildren's parents (Fortes 1949: 236–240).

While several of the authors here reproduce the image of sympathy and intimacy, the pictures they paint are more complicated. Van der Geest's account from an Akan-speaking town in Ghana describes reciprocity with an emphasis on the performance of respect by grandchildren, especially toward their grandfathers. The conventional image of warmth and rich intimate interchange seems to fit better the relations between grandmothers and small children than that between older ones and grandfathers. The behaviour of an old man to his granddaughter is described as 'peevish and mean', though he jokingly called her his 'wife'. It is only the grandfather who jokes, whereas the child keeps respectfully silent, and one imagines her hurrying away from the hut of the old man after having finished her household duties for him.

Geissler and Prince, writing about Kenyan Luo grandmothers, propose that the notion of sharing captures the quality of relations to grandchildren more accurately than that of reciprocity. They describe the sharing of time and lived-in space, food, bodily touch and modes of address, which imply 'shared' modes of personhood. The contrasting interpretations—Van der Geest pointing to seemingly 'empty' performances of respect while Geissler and Prince underline closeness and sharing of substances—may have to do with real differences between an Akan trading community and a Luo agricultural one. But they may also be related to the difference between grandmothers and grandfathers, or that between small grandchildren and older ones. Moreover, they might be less contradictory than they seem, as a general emphasis on practices of substantial relatedness does not preclude conflicts and tensions within social relations. As Van der Geest suggests, these apparent contradictions may be rooted in the difference between image or rhetoric about respect and real practice. The way Van der Geest's young men talk about the importance of their grandfathers is contrasted by their everyday lack of interest in them.

The phenomenology of relational qualities features in the contributions of Notermans, Geissler and Prince, and Whyte and Whyte. Descriptions of familiar interactions—touch, sharing of food and bed, talking together—give a sense of immediacy to accounts of the quality of relationships. The anthropologist's appreciation of these feelings and practices comes clearly through. Looking back we can recognise it in the evocative descriptions by Fortes of Tallensi grandparents and grandchildren, but it is even richer in the contemporary ethnography.

This new attention not only to everyday practices, but also in a very concrete sense to the substances shared by or flowing between relatives, links our collection of articles to the new kinship debates which conceptualise kinship as 'relatedness'. The idea is that relationships should be seen as 'constructed through everyday practice' rather than given by an imagined 'nature' or the formal existence of kinship ties (Carsten 2000: 17). A key position in this concept of relatedness, and in some of our articles, is the perception of 'biological' substances as symbolising relatedness between people. Several of our contributions go further. In contrast to the notion that milk and breast-feeding symbolise mother-hood in Africa, Notermans shows that 'real motherhood' means to share a bed and to sleep together. This is the noted practice of Batouri grand-mothers reclaiming grandchildren as their children. Geissler and Prince propose an even wider notion of 'shared substance', which includes not only food and bodily contact, but also the shared life force that ances-tral names and particularly common relational address and nicknaming evoke. This 'flows' together with the other material substances within the small practices and gestures of everyday life between persons.

LIFETIMES

Temporality was a concern of the early work on grandparents in at least two ways. Radcliffe-Brown (1950) pointed to a kind of structural time, in which a generation is replaced not by the immediately succeeding one, but by the generation of grandchildren. Biological time and its link to the developmental cycle of domestic groups provided another angle on generational relations. Goody (1966) and others drew attention to the processes of growth and decline in household size and composition, as children were born, grew up to establish new homes, and parents aged.

Whyte and Whyte trace these cyclical processes over thirty years in a village in eastern Uganda, showing how the pattern of living with grandchildren is affected by long-term cycles and not only by historical transformations. Their article draws attention to the methodological difficulties of distinguishing between cyclical changes and historical transformations. Comparing the quantitative data of two generations, they argue, could be easily interpreted as historical change, whereas in comparison with a third generation the change seems to be a cyclical fluctuation. This methodological difficulty is, of course, due to our own limited lifetime and research possibilities which make it difficult for us to do research over more lifetimes than our own.

However, it is historical processes and their effect upon relations between grandparents and grandchildren that preoccupy many scholars today. Planners and policy makers in countries hard hit by the AIDS epi-demic are concerned about the 'orphan crisis' and the burdens it places upon grandparents (Nyambedha *et al.* 2003). Ingstad provides examples from Botswana, where HIV prevalence is one of the highest in the world. Like Whyte and Whyte, she points out that the effects of AIDS are com-pounded by other factors. In Botswana labour migration and the increas-ing number of children born out of wedlock are also changing the situa-tion of grandparents. She shows how the meaning of grandparenthood is being undermined by the epidemic and by these other forces. Instead of enjoying dignity and respect, grandparents face loss, overwhelming responsibilities, and lack of resources. Her argument is that quali-ties of relationship between grandparents and grandchildren must be understood in historical time and in relation to these patterns of change.

From Benin, Alber describes a contrasting historical transformation. Whereas grandparents in Botswana are increasingly caring for grand-children, those in northern Benin are doing so rather less, as the institution of fostering children declines. Urban migration seems to be the key here; town parents tend not to send their children to the country to be fostered by grandparents. In this case too, grandparents experience a moral loss because of the social value that fostering gave them.

Most of the contributions trace the ways in which people experience and express their sense of broad historical changes. An idealised past is opposed to present reality in some situations, but, as the article by Geissler and Prince shows, grandmothers also embrace modernity in many ways, and some of them construct their identity as well as their relations to grandchildren in terms of radical discontinuity with the past. It is not simply the case that grandparents are icons of the past, or that they imagine change as only negative.

Time as lived with others is a theme in the contributions of Notermans and Whyte and Whyte. The life trajectories that Notermans describes in Cameroon are those of social, not individual, actors. A woman's life course towards grandmotherhood is intertwined with the reproductive trajectory of her parents and children, especially her daughters. In eastern Uganda, the quality of relations to grandchildren are understood in terms of lives lived with the parents of those grandchildren, as well as with the grandchildren themselves. Whyte and Whyte use the concept of intersubjective time to capture the ways that relationships are made by shared past experience and imaginations of intertwined futures with children, grandchildren and in-laws.

Taken together the six articles assembled here give rich pictures of the relations between grandparents and grandchildren from across the continent. They show how one of the most fundamental of family relations is lived out and experienced in different societies. And they demonstrate how historical consciousness, on the part of researchers and the social actors they study, affects the understanding of these relations.

REFERENCES

Carsten, J. 2000. 'Introduction: cultures of relatedness', in J. Carsten (ed.), *Cultures of Relatedness: new approaches to the study of kinship*. Cambridge: Cambridge University Press.

Fortes, M. 1949. *The Web of Kinship among the Tallensi: the second part of an analysis of the social structure of a Trans-Volta tribe*. London: Oxford University Press, for the International African Institute.

Goody, J. (ed.). 1966. (1958). *The Developmental Cycle in Domestic Groups*. Cambridge: Cambridge University Press.

Johnson-Hanks, J. 2002. 'On the limits of life stages in ethnography: toward a theory of vital conjunctures', *American Anthropologist* 104 (3): 865–80.

Nyambedha, E. O., S. Wandibba, and J. Aagaard-Hansen. 2003. 'Changing patterns of orphan care due to the HIV epidemic in western Kenya', *Social Science and Medicine* 57 (2): 301–11.

Radcliffe-Brown, A. R. 1950. 'Introduction', in A. R. Radcliffe-Brown and D. Forde (eds), *African Systems of Kinship and Marriage*. London: Oxford University Press, for the International African Institute.

SHARING HOME, FOOD, AND BED: PATHS OF GRANDMOTHERHOOD IN EAST CAMEROON

Catrien Notermans

Throughout my fieldwork in a provincial town in East Cameroon I followed the life of Marie-Lucie. When I first met her in 1993, she was thirty-three years old and having a sexual relationship with the prospect of having more children. When I met her for the last time in Cameroon in 2000, she was forty years old and calling herself *une vieille femme* because 'she did not sleep with men any more'. Now, as a 43-year-old woman, she is worrying about her death and the possible futures of her children.[1] Despite her 'advanced age' she leads a dynamic life. She cultivates a field of cassava, peanuts, and vegetables in the vicinity of the kindergarten where she works as a teacher for a low, irregularly paid salary. She needs to do both the agricultural and the wage work since she is responsible for four biological children, on average six foster-children, and two grandchildren. She gives herself to all these children but enthusiastically celebrates the presence of her two grandchildren: a four-year-old girl and a one-year-old boy.

The celebration of these two grandchildren sharply contrasts with the indifference that she displayed towards her last-born biological child during my second fieldwork in 1996. She deliberately neglected this child when he was three months old and fell ill. She did not make any attempt to keep him alive as he reminded her of a badly ended relationship and she felt too old to care for children born from relationships that had already been broken off. Moreover, it was time for her sixteen-year-old daughter to bear children. Within a year of her baby's death, her aged mother also died and then Marie-Lucie resolutely decided to stop her sexual and reproductive trajectory and to permit her daughter to start hers. Rather than uttering threats to punish her for falling pregnant, she encouraged her daughter to have a baby and allowed her to stop taking the usual contraceptive injections. When her first granddaughter was born, Marie-Lucie immediately claimed her and raised her as if she were her own child. Three years later, she also claimed the newborn grandson from her daughter who had to give in to her request without complaint. When I ask her now how her grandchildren are doing, she expresses her warmth and intimacy towards them by saying: 'Cathie, they are fine, we share the same bed.'

CATRIEN NOTERMANS is lecturer and senior researcher in the Department of Cultural Anthropology of the University of Nijmegen in the Netherlands. Since 1992, she has researched into gender, marriage, religion and childhood in Cameroon. Her 1999 Ph.D. was awarded for a thesis on Cameroonian Christian women in polygynous marriages. Her current research involves child fosterage both in Cameroon and on Marian pilgrimage in France.

[1] It is important to note that in Cameroon, female life expectancy at birth is 55.23 years (World Factbook 2002: Cameroon).

From a Western kinship perspective, these grandchildren are not her 'own' children, though for Marie-Lucie they certainly are. Her daughter breast-fed the babies, but she did not attain the status of motherhood since Marie-Lucie confiscated the children for herself through sleeping with them and not allowing the fathers to recognise the children. Marie-Lucie thoroughly enjoys her status of grandmother, a status she purposefully realised by ending her own sexual and reproductive life. Though being a mother and being a grandmother feel different for Marie-Lucie, the daily practice of grandmotherhood seems not to differ greatly from motherhood since she disciplines her grandchildren in the same way as she disciplines her biological and foster-children; and it is she who pays for clothes, school fees, and medical care. The grandchildren call her *maman* and their biological mother *tantine* ('aunty'), which illustrates that they do not experience generational differences between their social and their biological mother. This characteristic of generational relations is also found elsewhere in the region.

Ruel (2002: 52) states that in many West African societies the dominant model for relations between generations is the dyadic one of parents to children: relations between members of alternate generations are not contrasted with those between members of adjacent generations but rather assimilated to them. Sangree (1974) also notices that in West Africa relationships between grandparents and grandchildren become indistinguishable from the usual parent–child relationship and that children often speak of their grandmothers as their 'real' mothers since it was the grandmother who brought them up and whom they most respected. Both authors observe that such usages would be unthinkable for many East African people who always distinguish sharply between kin of the parental and grandparental generations.

In this article, I will argue that grandmotherhood and motherhood, though being fluid categories, are differently performed and experienced. I will also argue that grandmotherhood is not a uniform life stage but that women follow different trajectories to achieve it. Though Marie-Lucie's trajectory represents many other women's life courses, it does not correspond to all since women make different choices among the possibilities or 'horizons' (Johnson-Hanks 2002) the local marriage and kinship system offers them. To elaborate women's trajectories into grandmotherhood I will apply Johnson-Hanks' argument (*op. cit.*) for a new anthropology of the life course and argue that women's lives are dynamically enacted and organised in ways not bound to stages. Life stages, such as grandmotherhood, are not inevitably undergone but have to be actively chosen and performed in order to be gained.

With a focus on the performing aspects of grandmotherhood, I will also illustrate how grandmothers operate in the matrilineal descent system. Though Eurocentric and androcentric biases in West European kinship theories have already been challenged by a number of anthropologists (Bouquet 1993; Carsten 2000; Holy 1996: Schneider 1984; Schweitzer 2000; Stone 2000), I will add that African kinship systems have been misconstrued through neglecting grandmothers' agency in the domain of descent. In contrast with a West European stereotype view of grandmothers as a category of inactive marginal old women, grandmothers in East Cameroon play an important part in decision processes and strongly influence matters of descent.

MULTIPLE CHOICES, MULTIPLE PATHS

Authors like Bledsoe (2002) and Johnson-Hanks (2002) have recently critiqued the strong form of the life cycle model since vital life events are rarely coherent, clear in direction, or fixed in outcome. Johnson-Hanks (*op. cit.*: 865) criticises the model from her fieldwork in southern Cameroon and illustrates that, rather than a clear trajectory toward adulthood or parenthood, people follow multiple and variable paths and that the pace of trajectories varies not only between people but also for an individual (*op. cit.*: 868). I will follow the same argument with regard to the status of grandmotherhood. Grandmotherhood is not a single status but can differ considerably from woman to woman and also within a woman.

Women in East Cameroon have to deal with a multiplicity of practices of marriage and descent that are highly fluid, flexible, and negotiable. They constantly shape and reshape their life in a society where matrilineal descent is closely interconnected with patrilineal descent, formal polygyny, informal polygyny (men's practice of having informal marriages with 'outside wives' [Karanja 1987, 1994; Mann 1994]), and informal polyandry (women's practice of having informal marriages with 'outside husbands' [Guyer 1994; Notermans 1999]). This complexity of different practices creates a wide range of choices for all persons involved. Women select and pursue different possibilities simultaneously and successively at different moments of life. Their choices are never made 'forever' but for the time being they create good opportunities. Theoretical models are often too rigid and categorical to capture women's continual reinterpretation and reshaping of previously chosen paths in which different agents, such as mothers, husbands and husbands' relatives also participate and decide.

Instead of the life stage model that neglects interdependent agency (Piot 1999), multiple individual trajectories, and the changeableness of life courses, Johnson-Hanks (2002: 872) proposes a model of 'vital conjunctures' that have duration and multiple outcomes over different time frames. Johnson-Hanks describes vital conjunctures as 'experiential knots during which potential futures are under debate and up for grabs' and calls these imagined futures 'the horizons of the conjuncture':

> These horizons are specific to a time: what looks like a hopeful prospect now may be closed down without warning tomorrow, and another potential future may open up. They are also specific to a perspective or agent position. Conjunctures are navigated in reference to their horizons. Although the conjunctures and their horizons are variable, actor's orientations to them are

often systematic since their forms of imagination belong to the social field. [*ibid.*]

Women in East Cameroon often experience several vital conjunctures simultaneously or successively in relatively short periods during which they have to make well-considered decisions about different trajectories. When falling pregnant, do they want to keep the child, do they want to marry the father, are they willing to accept one or more co-wives, do they want to move to the husband's family, or do they only want the father to sign the birth certificate? When a daughter gets pregnant, should she be allowed to keep the child, which possible persons will claim the child, in what ways will she earn the money to raise the child, does she have to accept marriage or not, will she be her husband's first or his second wife? For all these questions, women do not have clear solutions but have to find the answer in 'navigating the horizons' that are available to them in the given social context. While navigating they sometimes have to rely on the decisions relatives make for them, sometimes they can make the decisions themselves or in dialogue with others but for all decisions it can be said that they are reinterpretable and changeable over time.

The vital conjuncture mentioned in the introduction lasted about one year. It opened when Marie-Lucie was already pregnant and had been left by the father of the child; it developed when the baby was born and fell ill. Marie-Lucie navigated the possible horizons, refused the horizon of being an abandoned mother and decided to let the baby die. Then, her mother suddenly died. Marie-Lucie felt it her responsibility to replace her mother in the lineage and finally chose the horizon of being a grandmother. Though many other people were involved in these dramatic events—the father of her child who deceived her, her child who fell ill, her mother who died, her daughter who wanted to have a sexual relationship—she actively created her own future: that of a proud and respectable grandmother.

MARRIAGE AND DESCENT: THE SOCIAL FIELD

Before entering into different paths and performances of grand-motherhood, I will first describe the social field from which women choose their paths to become mothers or grandmothers. Since 1992 I have been doing fieldwork in Batouri, first on polygyny and more recently on women's and children's experiences with fosterage.[2] Batouri is a small provincial town of 25,000 inhabitants in the savannah area in East Cameroon, 500 kilometres distant from the capital Yaoundé.

---

[2] This article is based on long periods of anthropological fieldwork in Cameroon between 1992 and 2000. These periods extended over two, twelve, two and six months successively. WOTRO (Netherlands Foundation for the Advancement of Tropical Research), the Department of Anthropology and the Centre for Gender Studies at the University of Nijmegen financially supported the research.

Fieldwork focused on the part of the town called Mbondossi, inhabited by about 1,500 people. Most are Kako, but members of other ethnic groups of the Eastern province in Cameroon, such as the Yangélé and the Byemo, also consider Mbondossi their home. For most people, urban life is continually linked to family life in the native villages, largely through children who regularly move between kin in town and the surrounding villages.

Women in the district enjoy social respect and a quite independent position in relation to men through monopolising the production, marketing and preparation of food. As the story of Marie-Lucie illustrated, grandmothers also belong to the category of active farmers. Women may choose to be grandmothers from their mid-thirties but that does not mean that they rest on their laurels for the remainder of their life. Even at an advanced age, women continue cultivating their fields to have food to share with their children. They do not willingly abandon their fields as both food and the sharing of it are vital elements in maintaining and creating social relationships, which are crucial for having the feeling of 'being alive'. Men, in general, do not assist in food production but strive to have a job to earn money for maintaining their families. In this, however, they hardly succeed owing to high unemployment rates in Cameroon.

In spite of financial shortcomings, men generally marry several wives: one quarter of the households in the district are formally polygynous and almost all these marriages include an average number of two co-wives. People point out that polygyny is more frequently practised than official statistics reveal because monogamous marriages appear to be informally polygynous in daily practice. Men prefer to marry one woman formally and to combine this marriage with a number of mistresses or 'outside wives' since such an informal polygynous relationship is considered cheaper than assuming full responsibility for several wives and their children. Women, for their part, also combine formal marriage with a number of informal conjugal relationships. They feel free to have different sexual relationships simultaneously and/or successively, and men take it for granted as women take polygyny for granted. In local language, extramarital relationships for both men and women, are called *wanja*.

Women do not value marriage highly: they readily divorce or leave their husband for a while. Neither marriage nor husbands are at the centre of women's interest. Copet-Rougier (1985, 1987) argues that this attitude towards marriage arose in the 1970s when women began to challenge male structures of dominance and gradually changed stable marriages into 'marriages of trial'. Most of women's trajectories are not directed towards marriage since women's ambition is to secure independence and marital flexibility rather than a stable marriage. High flexibility of marriages is possible due to the low value of bridewealth that nowadays is often not even transferred. Women's relatives rarely insist on receiving bridewealth as that would give the father a claim on the children. This results in a high frequency of informal marital relationships, for men as well as for women, that are said to be 'marriages' but have not been confirmed with bridewealth or a marriage certificate. If a *wanja* relationship has lasted for more than one year, people define it as 'marriage' since the exchange of food, money and sex is at the core of both marital and *wanja* relationships.

It is not shameful for women to give birth to children in different marriages. On the contrary, it seems to be their aim. Even when women themselves do not strive for it intentionally, their mothers may urge them to have some children from informal relationships in order to claim the children for themselves. Marie-Lucie gave birth to four children from four different fathers in four different relationships, of which only one had been a formal marriage. Her mother repeatedly prevented her from marriage and made her own husband (Marie-Lucie's father) sign the birth certificates in order to keep Marie-Lucie's children in the matrilineage. This was also the case with Marie-Lucie's sisters for whom their father also signed the children's birth certificates. When her daughter gave birth to her grandchildren, Marie-Lucie acted in the same way as her mother did before: she did not allow her daughter to get married and claimed the children.

This attitude with respect to marriages and children has to be understood in relation to the descent system. Though Kako society, in anthropological literature, has always been characterised as male-dominated, polygynous and patrilineal (Copet 1977; Copet-Rougier 1985, 1987), matrilineages do exist side by side with patrilineages. Women's contributions to their matrilineages are closely linked to polyandrous relationships that, due to gender-blindness, have also been overlooked in previous research in the area. Moreover, grandmothers have been ignored as important agents in matters of descent. Young fathers, rather than elderly women, were the centre of interest as it was supposed that they would claim their children.

Grandmothers mostly claim their daughters' children by preventing the children's fathers from transferring bridewealth or signing a birth certificate. As women do not easily enter into formal marriages, men often have to claim their children through signing birth certificates. However, they are powerless in cases where maternal grandmothers make the claim. Fathers offer little or no resistance to maternal grandmothers who are powerful actors in the matrilineage and whose decisions have to be respected. Grandmothers' claims also release them from paying for cloth and medicine and from paying fees in the future. Especially young fathers often cannot meet these costs and easily give in when others are ready to accept responsibility. Fathers also often refuse to recognise their children and to shoulder the burden of financial support since they also bear responsibility for children of their unmarried sisters.

In some cases, rather than preventing a father from signing the birth, the grandmother may force him to sign the certificate in order to hold him responsible for financial support and make him pay for the baby's layette and the first medical care. However, in these cases, grandmothers often will not allow the father to take the children with him and insist on keeping the children within the maternal household.

At the same time, grandmothers will keep the birth certificate in their possession. They are able to tear it up when the child has successfully survived her/his first years of life and medical costs become less risky. After having destroyed the first certificate, grandmothers are allowed to register the child again and to identify a male member of the maternal family as the child's father. Even when a grandmother allows the father to sign the birth certificate, she will often arrange for a second birth certificate to be issued in which a mother's brother, the mother's father, or a deceased husband is recorded as the child's father. But this may have consequences when the biological father who financially supported his child for years is not willing to give up his rights.

People who feel powerless in the domains of kinship and marriage can ask for help at the provincial department of the Ministry of Social Affairs in Batouri. Most problems discussed at this ministry relate to the multiplicity of children's birth certificates and concern fathers who accuse their children's maternal family of having taken the children away. Women rarely need to ask civil servants for help concerning arguments about rights on children, as they have a more powerful position in these matters. To resolve the quarrels presented at the ministry, the civil servant acts according to local notions of kinship by not considering biological fatherhood to be the decisive factor but by finding out who 'suffered' most for the children through daily care and financial support and who invested most in them through the sharing of food and home. All these gestures and problems concerning birth certificates that are negotiated, signed, changed, contested, destroyed, or returned express people's flexible and changeable attitudes towards descent.

It is not easy to categorise these attitudes through standard anthropological frameworks. Theories of descent have played a vital part in the history of anthropology, though for the most part, they have only concentrated on unilineal descent as true descent (Parkin 1997: 143). This unilineal bias, emphasising patriliny in particular, has been so influential that ethnographic studies have to re-examine and reclassify societies that previously were characterised as unilineal. Recently published studies on Cameroon call for such a deconstruction of traditional typologies and advance the existence of matrilineages in societies where previously only partilineages had been identified (see Feldman-Savelsberg 1996; Gausset 1998). While both Feldman-Savelsberg and Gausset explain the descent systems in question as being double unilineal, this is not the case in East Cameroon where children at birth are not recruited in both unilineal groups of descent at the same time. Though patrilineages and matrilineages coexist, children belong to one or the other: group membership is not automatically given but has to be discussed and negotiated. Parents often say that their children are *entre nous* ('in between') to express that definitive outcomes are not yet sure. In the negotiations that follow grandmothers strongly influence the decisions to be made.

When taking all women's different trajectories into account—including non-marital relationships, pre-marital relationships, marital relationships, multiple marital relationships, post-marital relationships, temporarily without marital relationships and definitively without marital relationships—and the trajectories of grandmothers in particular, matrilineal descent comes up as dominant. Out of all relationships women enter into, they generally accept only one to be a formal marriage in which they move to their husband's place and give up their rights in biological children in exchange for goods, money, and social respect. An often-heard argument for doing so is that suffering for a husband and his family makes a woman a 'good' woman. A husband has to compensate for his wife's suffering and reproduction of children and is expected to make a valuable financial contribution to his wife's family. When the husband fails to do so, women speak about 'wasting their time' and take the matter to court to claim damages for *le temps perdu*.

Because women enter into marriage mainly for reasons of financial benefit and social status they will resolutely bring their marriage to an end when reciprocity fails. Marriage is not considered an easy trajectory because it is during formal marriage that a woman has to deal with her husband's lineages (both his patrilineage and his matrilineage) who claim their children born in marriage. Before, during, and after this period of belonging to a patrilocal and male-dominated household, women mainly work on their matrilineage through fostering children and bearing children from plural informal relationships while staying at their mother's or brother's place.

What was previously recognised as patrilineal descent in Batouri (Copet 1977; Copet-Rougier 1985, 1987) consists in present-day urban society of bridewealth and patrilocal residence for the time marriage lasts.[3] It is even questionable whether these customs prove the existence of extensive patrilineages, as married men often place their legitimate children in the charge of their sisters, who are either barren or deprived of biological children through divorce. It is even striking how vulnerable male-dominated, patrilocal households are and how often they are the target of violent witchcraft attacks. Due to weak conjugal bonds that are the base of these households, and due to minimal trust and solidarity between spouses, between co-wives, and between children of different co-wives, these households easily collapse when hostility is no longer bearable. When social relationships and places become 'sick', people feel ill themselves and will abandon the household to recover.

Taking all these aspects into account, the descent system can be considered a dominantly matrilineal one in which men occasionally have the possibility to claim children through practices such as transferring bridewealth and signing birth certificates. This enables them to create

---

[3] I assume that discrepancies between data collected in the 1970s and the 1990s partly result from historical changes in the marriage and descent system in East Cameroon, and partly from changes in anthropological approaches, premises, and concepts. Recent anthropological studies that challenge previous ethnocentric and androcentric biases in approaches of descent and do not take marriage as women's central and most important trajectory, produce divergent results; but also historical changes such as urbanisation and an increasing number of female-headed households in town affect people's attitudes to marriage and descent.

households that are dominated by brothers and sons and to supply their matrilineage with children. These practices engender for the woman a more vulnerable and less powerful position as formal marriage implies that she loses her children after divorce and also runs the risk of losing them in the course of marriage when her husband's sisters claim the children. However, she may counterbalance this loss of biological children through claiming foster-children from her brothers (Notermans 2003).

The co-existence of matri- and patrilineal descent came to the fore in my research on fosterage in particular, since the high frequency of child fosterage in the area appeared to be closely linked to practices of matrilineal descent. Children in Batouri frequently reside in a household other than that of their biological mother. A survey held in 1999 in the district Mbondossi, revealed that 31% of the children lived with foster-parents. Children can be fostered by men as well as women and mainly move to their maternal grandmother, their mother's brother or their father's sister. From first menstruation onwards, women are informed that they are going to bear children not for themselves but for the matrilineage and that lineage members may always ask for them. To be respected and full members in society, women have to share their children in the same way as they have to share their food. Women's production and cooking of food as well as women's bearing and rearing of children are used in creating and maintaining relationships. Much food and many children symbolise women's strength, as both are fundamentals in the realm of kin relationships.

SHARING HOME, FOOD, AND BED

In East Cameroon, people do not automatically become kin through biological ties. Social kinship (e.g. fosterage) is much more valued than biological kinship since social kinship—often translated as 'real' kinship—is based on personal offerings, mutual commitment and sharing. Kinship must be obtained, negotiated, fed and performed. Both physical proximity and the sharing of food are closely linked to notions of kinship and central to performances of grandmotherhood. Grandchildren who live far away do not make a woman a grandmother, but grandchildren who share home, food and bed with her undoubtedly do. This sharing points to a relational commitment between grandmothers and grand-children in which the grandmother cooks for her grandchildren, feeds them, physically devotes herself to them, and in which the grandchildren help their grandmother with all kinds of domestic tasks, give her social respect, continue her lineage and guarantee future remembrance.

Grandmothers consider their commitment to grandchildren a stage of life that succeeds the stage of being sexually active. When Marie-Lucie declares that she shares her bed with her grandchildren, she also declares that 'she does not sleep with men any more'. With this statement she refers to both similarities and differences between 'sleeping with grandchildren' and 'sleeping with men'. As mothers, women share food and bed also with men but in a more calculated and reciprocal way: a wife cooks for her husband, sleeps with him and expects to get money and gifts in return. When food and sex are not reciprocated women do not hesitate to end the relationship. This balanced reciprocity sharply contrasts with the sharing of bed and food between grandmothers and grandchildren as the latter is disconnected from the right to receive. Woodburn's argument (1998) that 'sharing is not a form of exchange' rightly applies to the practice of sharing in performances of grandmotherhood: children and food have to be shared without binding the recipient to reciprocate.

Grandmothers' sleeping with grandchildren also differs from sharing practices in mother–child relationships. In grandmother–grandchildren relationships the sharing of bed and food lasts much longer. Children usually enjoy the intimacy of sleeping together with their biological mother only throughout the period that the mother breast-feeds them. Then, sharing the bed also implies that the mother has no sexual relationships and completely devotes herself to her children. This physical devotion and intimacy does often not last for more than two years. Mothers who breast-feed their babies for longer periods voluntarily renounce the possibility of having new sexual affairs. As Maher (1995: 16) argues, with long periods of breast-feeding, women emphasise their role as mothers and kinswomen at the expense of their conjugal relationship.

When children are weaned at the age of two, they are supposed to speak, to walk and to get into the habit of executing commissions for their (grand)parents. Then, their mothers are allowed to reclaim their independence and to take up their sexual and reproductive trajectories. This means that babies cannot sleep in their mother's bed and suckle at night. From weaning onwards, children get used to a hierarchical relationship with their mother that disallows public expressions of mother's emotional and physical commitment to the children. There is no play, no talk, no cuddle; the relationship is one of authority and obedience. In this way children learn to be emotionally independent of the mother and to fit in a wider network of kin who care for them.

Breast-feeding and sexual activity do not harmonise for at least two other reasons. First, there is the often-mentioned awareness that new pregnancies will spoil the mother's breast milk and that the breast-fed baby will be at risk of dying. Second, women who engage in sexual relationships are not '*calmes*'; concerns about marriage require a lot of time and flexibility in which young children would stand in the way. It is said that emotional and physical intimacy in the mother–child relationship through breast-feeding obstructs women on their reproductive and marital paths, as these demand a lot of flexibility and often force women to leave their children with matrilineal kin. Through weaning, new trajectories can be opened in which children from previous relationships do not fit.

Not only do women perform grandmotherhood differently from motherhood, children also experience grandmother's motherhood as highly different from mother's motherhood. Grandmothers are '*calmes*' and '*sur place*'; they no longer move between different sexual relation-ships or marriages, they are not bothered with unfaithful husbands or jealous co-wives, they have time to set up an intimate relationship and they are not overly demanding; grandmothers sleep with their grand-children for long periods of time and that is why children say that 'grand-mothers are mothers but distinct ones'. Marie-Lucie's grandchildren consider their grandmother to be their 'real' mother as she feeds them and sleeps with them. However, by having access to their grandmother's bed and physical warmth, they occupy a privileged position among the other (biological and foster-) children in the household. Marie-Lucie does not share her bed with her biological and foster-children, first, because these children are already beyond the age of sharing a bed, and second, because they belong to the category 'children' rather than 'grandchildren' and for reasons of authority and discipline, mothers do not aim at sharing their bed with their children for a long time.

Children who live with grandmothers say that they also live calmly themselves. They will not be as easily abandoned by their 'mother' as children living with married mothers are. As marriage—characterised by competition between both spouses and co-wives, by witchcraft accusations and by frequent divorces or temporary separations—is one of women's most important motives behind fostering their children with kin, the absence of their grandmother's 'sleeping with men' prevents children from being abandoned. Grandchildren who share home, food, and bed with their grandmother do not have to compete with fathers or stepfathers who favour their (biological) children or their sisters' and brothers' children. Since all these politics of power are absent in the grandmother–grandchildren relationships, both are able to fully enjoy it.

The intensity of sharing home, food, and bed with grandchildren varies in different paths of grandmotherhood. In line with Johnson-Hanks' model of vital conjunctures (2002), I want to advance in the next sections that women in East Cameroon do not have a clear trajectory toward grandmotherhood but follow different paths at different moments of time. This means that relationships with grandchildren vary between women and over the life of an individual. Differences between women arise from different choices made by different women and from different positions in the maternal household. Differences within an individual life course arise from both women's own multiple positions towards marriage and the different positions their children (the grandchildren's parents) take towards marriage, successively and simultaneously. When considering all possible different trajectories, it becomes evident that the full sharing of home, food, and bed, as described in the case of Marie-Lucie, represents an ideal realisation of grandmotherhood that cannot be reached by all grandmothers or in all paths of grandmotherhood equally.

PATHS OF GRANDMOTHERHOOD: DIFFERENCES WITHIN A LIFE COURSE

In my focus on multiple paths of grandmotherhood I share Moore's 'passion for difference' (1993, 1994). She argues that lives are shaped by a multiplicity of differences, which may be perceived categorically but are lived relationally. Though, in the next two sections, I will draw boundaries between different categories of grandmothers and grandchildren, I agree with Moore that differences are not as categorical as anthropologists would often like it. Analytical boundaries do not reflect synchronised complexity and historical flexibility in women's lives where boundaries are flexible, changeable and negotiable and move in the same way as the people move. In focusing on differences within life courses I join Johnson-Hanks' and Bourdieu's call to reintroduce time into theoretical representations (Johnson-Hanks 2002; Bourdieu 1977). I will illustrate that trajectories of motherhood and grandmotherhood unfold and change in time. Though rights in children are discussed after birth, changes in people's life courses lead to resumption of negotiations on descent. The outcomes of these renewed negotiations may alter grandmothers' relationships with grandchildren through their life.

Within an individual life course, women have different relationships with different grandchildren. Both grandmother's own and her children's flexible positions towards marriage make these differences. Relationships with grandchildren born to children they had within marriage will differ from relationships with grandchildren born to children they had outside marriage. As women have full rights to children born from informal marriages, from birth onwards the relationships with these children's children will be strongest. As the children born from marriage do not belong to their mother but to her husband, relationships with these children's children will be less intensive, at least in the first years after birth. If a woman is still in a marriage and sexually active when her first grandchildren are born, her relationship with these grandchildren will also be less intensive. However, since the full sharing of home, food, and bed becomes possible when a woman ceases to sleep with a man, a grandmother may choose to leave the conjugal household to fully enjoy her grandmotherhood. She may also distance herself from husband and co-wives by constructing a small accommodation at the margin of the husband's courtyard or near to it. This is possible because a married woman is hardly ever her husband's only wife. Especially at an advanced age, when married women often feel (sexually and financially) abandoned by their husband and replaced by a younger co-wife, women may prefer to live with their grandchildren.

Differences within grandmothers' life courses also arise from their children's trajectories and multiple positions towards marriage. Daughters and sons show a continually flexible attitude to marriage and their trajectories strongly influence relationships between alternate generations. Children provide their mother with grandchildren born in marriage as well as with grandchildren born outside marriage. While grandmothers hardly differentiate between grandsons and granddaughters, they do have different relationships with children of married sons, children of unmarried sons, children of married daughters and children of unmarried daughters. Women's relationships with these different categories of grandchildren, moreover, vary in time. Women's daughters who are actually married can be divorced later on, and the other way round. Also women's sons who are actually married can be left without wives in time. As marriage changes rapidly and regularly for all persons involved, grandmothers' relationships with grandchildren may also change over time.

Grandmothers have fewest intensive and intimate relationships with children of unmarried sons since the mother's matrilineal kin generally claim these children. Grandmothers often relate to children of unmarried sons as they relate to children of married daughters: they are not allowed to claim them immediately. Children of married daughters belong to their father's lineages and are supposed to live with him. As long as the father keeps his children, the maternal grandmother will mostly invest less time and intimacy in relationships with these children. The sharing of home, food, and bed is not up to them, unless the father's lineages do not care well for them and neglect them.

For example, in the event of co-wife rivalry in their father's home, mothers or the children themselves can initiate fosterage. They can decide to leave the household, to look for better circumstances, and to live with the maternal grandmother. When subsequently a relationship of trust and affection has been established through the sharing of home, food, and bed or through less intensive performances of grandmotherhood, grandmothers will not easily abandon them or give them back to their father's lineages. Then, food kinship has been generated and that is considered stronger than kinship based on blood, bridewealth or birth certificate.

Though children of married sons belong to their paternal grand-mother's lineage, paternal grandmothers initially do not live with these children nor claim them. When sons marry they usually leave their mother's place but will often foster their children with sisters 'from the same womb' who are left without children through divorce, husband's death, or infertility problems—brothers' wives have to accept this, as formal marriage deprives them of rights to biological children. A married son does not foster his children firstly with his mother but with his unmarried sisters; his mother may however enjoy the presence of his children after weaning or later on, because her unmarried daughters often live with her at her place.

Within the system of matrilineal descent, unmarried daughters are of special importance for mothers. These daughters live in their mother's place and have to give in to her claims on children. When grandmothers are not married (any more), as happened in the case of Marie-Lucie, a full sharing of home, food, and bed will take place when they claim their unmarried daughter's children. When these daughters get married later on and give birth to children, their mother's relationships with these children will be different from their mother's relationships with their children born from informal marriages. However, in later stages of life, vital conjunctures in daughters' lives—concerning co-wife rivalry, conjugal separation or divorce—can lead to changes in these relationships.

In all these different relationships with different grandchildren, aspects of grandmotherhood are regularly performed to express strong bonds between grandmothers and grandchildren, even if the full sharing of home, food, and bed is not possible. These performances particularly reflect the special relationship daughters have with their mother, even when they do not live together at their mother's place. Throughout all the different trajectories of marriage and motherhood, daughters regularly come back to their mother's place, either for short or for long periods of time. When husbands do not behave properly, women return to their mother or brothers to display dissatisfaction about their husband and to wait for negotiations. During pregnancy daughters also usually return for long periods of time to their mother's kitchen in order to deliver there. Though in present-day urban society, women can also be sent to hospital for delivery, they often give birth in their mother's kitchen to express strong matrilineal ties.

Matrifocal households in town as well as in the surrounding villages are centred around the mother's kitchen in which the hearth symbolises her warmth, womb and solidarity (Feldman-Savelsberg 1996). As I mentioned before, cooking and eating are crucial forms of expressing relationships in general and of maintaining matrilineal ties in particular. Through giving birth to children in their grandmother's kitchen, mothers confirm that their children belong to their maternal family. Even when daughters are married, these practices express that a child's membership of the father's lineage does not exclude membership of the mother's lineage. When daughters give birth to their children at their mother's place, they also bury their children's umbilical cord at this place to express that their grandmother's home is their children's home whatever trajectory may be chosen and wherever it may end.

Women draw an analogy between the cooking of food and the cooking of children in the womb and, in both cooking and creating kinship ties, grandmothers appear to play a major role (see Feldman-Savelsberg 1996). Through feeding their daughters during pregnancy mothers contribute to the cooking of the child that grows in the womb. Grandmothers are considered specialists in cooking dishes that positively influence the development of the foetus. In general, women put a high value on the contribution of grandmother's food to the unborn child, more than on the contribution of the biological father's sperm as women mostly do not live with their husband but with their mother during pregnancy. It is especially through food that grandmothers may appropriate their grandchildren before delivery. The time and calmness they possess make them good cooks and givers of life par excellence. After delivery, women still spend some months with their mother being nursed and fed, as it is said that they also regain their strength from this.

When married daughters leave their mother's courtyard and take their baby back to their husband's home, they are very close to the child for the first two years till breastfeeding stops. Then, the child is often claimed by the maternal grandmother with whom it can have a good cry and accustom itself to separation from the mother. If the child is born from formal marriage, it will stay until the moment the father reclaims it. In that case, the child will leave the grandmother's place to join its parents but it will regularly come back for short visits or to spend whole school holidays. Even when grandmothers live in the villages and their grandchildren in town, they will invest in matrilineal kinship through claiming their grandchildren every now and then for sharing home, food, and bed together.

PATHS OF GRANDMOTHERHOOD: DIFFERENCES BETWEEN LIFE COURSES

In this section, I will focus on differences between grandmothers to clarify different trajectories that open, alternate, change, intensify or close over time and to illustrate that not only marital trajectories of sons and daughters affect trajectories of grandmotherhood, but also age hierarchies between siblings and grandmother's mother's agency.

Though Marie-Lucie's path to grandmotherhood is representative of many women, there are other different paths that women follow. Not all women have the opportunity, as Marie-Lucie has, to devote themselves totally to their grandchildren and to set up a relationship of sharing. Compared to other women in the district, Marie-Lucie proves to be a successful lineage head. At birth, she was her mother's second daughter and it was she who accompanied her elder sister into her marriage in order to help her and to give her weight at her husband's place. However, her elder sister died and then Marie-Lucie's trajectory changed. Now, it was Marie-Lucie who had to take care of her aged mother and who had to replace her. Her mother encouraged her to follow the paths of informal marriages rather than the path of formal marriage and made her husband sign her grandchildren's birth certificates. All through her life, marriage has been of little importance as she married only once and quickly divorced. Marie-Lucie was lucky that her second pregnancy resulted in the birth of a healthy daughter of whom she made an obedient and hardworking successor. Due to her central position in the maternal household, Marie-Lucie always expresses her willingness to receive the children of deceased and divorced brothers and sisters.

In the district, her household is a very special and respected one as she lives with her biological children, her foster-children and her grandchildren independently from others at her mother's place. Her salaried job has enabled her to construct a house with bricks and sheets of corrugated iron; and it still enables her to pay for electricity and running water and to repair material damages. Even when payments of salary are delayed, her job and the accompanying network of civil servants provide her with a strong position to negotiate credits that are often crucial to pay for her children's urgent medical care. All these privileges together make her powerful: she runs a household that is filled with children without depending on formal or informal husbands. Moreover, this autonomy makes her strong in negotiations about rights in children and birth certificates. To illustrate the differences between households, I will contrast the case of Marie-Lucie with the case of Emilienne.

Emilienne

Emilienne was 50 years old when I met her in 2000. Her mother had died several years ago and she never knew her father as her mother left him when she was still very young. Emilienne grew up with her mother and her mother's brother. She married but left her first husband after some years. She 'tried' two other marriages but finally came back to her mother's place. People told me that she had no biological children and only cared for several foster-children. She had, in fact, given birth to two children but neither Emilienne nor her foster-daughter ever mentioned these children as they were 'lost' after her divorce from her first husband. Emilienne returned to her mother's place in Mbondossi, where her elder sister was also living. This elder sister had also had different 'husbands' before returning to her mother. Emilienne's first foster-daughter gave her two grandchildren from informal marriages. During her daughter's third pregnancy, Emilienne approved her marriage to the father of the child and the daughter left home to join her new husband. Then, Emilienne moved with her three remaining foster-daughters to her brother's place, a village sixteen kilometres from town. Emilienne told me about her foster-children as follows:

> All of them are girls. I took the first one from my elder sister. Her first husband died but his family never claimed the children. She also gave birth to children before marriage. My sister gave all these children to our mother and joined her brother in Bertoua (a town eighty kilometres from Batouri). There she had several other 'husbands' but the children she received from them all belong to her since she consistently indicated her deceased husband as the biological father. I asked for one of these children when I left my husband and I felt too lonely. I have got my second foster-daughter from my brother. She was two years old when her mother left her father. I asked my brother for the child since my first (foster-) daughter was still too young to give me grandchildren. When she (the first [foster-] daughter) gave birth to her first child at the age of sixteen, I did not want her to marry the man who made her pregnant. I even prevented him from signing a birth certificate. It would enable him to claim his child one day and to take it away. In order to keep the child in the family my elder sister (the biological mother of the foster-daughter) declared her eldest son to be the father. That is what they wrote on the birth certificate. I brought this girl up as my own child. When her mother joined the father of her third child, I told her to leave my first granddaughter with me. Two years ago, I also asked my eldest (biological) son for his child. He received the child in an informal marriage and his 'wife' left him to join another husband. Both of them agreed to give me the girl. She is four years old now.

Emilienne's position in the matrilineage is not as strong as that of Marie-Lucie. It is not Emilienne but her elder sister who holds a strong position and who replaced their mother as the lineage head. Emilienne's elder sister gave birth to children in informal marriages before accepting a formal wedding. She even appropriated her biological children born in marriage and did not lose them in the same way as Emilienne did. After marriage, she successfully claimed her children from informal relationships through indicating her deceased husband as the biological father.

Not all women are equally successful in negotiating relations of marriage and descent. Those women who employ different strategies simultaneously and successively usually create the best circumstances and those who dedicate themselves totally to marriage are often less fortunate in having their 'own' children. However, a successful position in the lineage is influenced by a woman's fertility and the number of children she bears, as well as by her own agency in her marital trajectory. Emilienne, in contrast with her elder sister and Marie-Lucie, did not give birth to children in premarital relationships, nor in extra- and post-marital relationships. As her two biological children were given to her sister-in-law, she never managed to provide her matrilineage with biological children. However, though Emilienne's path started unsuccessfully, it later improved when her foster-daughter started her reproductive trajectory. When this daughter got pregnant, Emilienne immediately claimed the child and, after weaning, started sharing home, food, and bed. As she still has two foster-daughters who will bear children in time, her future may not be bad.

These alternating and unpredictable ways in which paths open and close, also concern Emilienne's two biological children. Though she had to abandon them after divorce and to accept not being in touch with them for years, her biological daughter finally came back to stay with her for some time and her biological son agreed to give her a granddaughter. It is not only grandmothers who have to navigate their horizons and make careful decisions; their children and, later on, their grandchildren may also navigate horizons and take paths that may change the life course of all persons involved.

The case also illustrates that age hierarchies among siblings influence the places of residence and paths of grandmotherhood. It is often the first-born daughter or the daughter who first succeeds in having children from informal marriages, who occupies her mother's place. When sons marry they settle elsewhere and the daughters who do not succeed their mother generally move between places of mother, brothers, formal husband and informal husbands. Emilienne moves between her mother's place in town, where her elder sister lives, and the place of her brother in the village. Though she regularly earns some money buying and selling vegetables, meat, and fish (the so-called *bayam salam*), she cannot afford to build a house for herself. This lack of sufficient income also makes her vulnerable in negotiations about rights in grandchildren. Since her first foster-daughter accepted marriage and gave birth to two children in this marriage, she never made any efforts to claim these children or to prevent their father from signing birth certificates. As her first foster-daughter found a good husband she even accepted that her first two granddaughters, born from informal marriages, moved to his place. Though she had already followed the path of grandmotherhood with the full sharing of home, food, and bed with her first two granddaughters, Emilienne now accepted being separated from her granddaughters. The paths that she follows now are the paths of her two remaining foster-daughters who will probably give her grandchildren in the course of time.

The case of Emilienne not only shows how paths can change throughout women's lives, but also how other people, and mothers in particular, can shape these paths. As well as the lack of plural marital relationships and the lack of many biological children, Emilienne has been less successful as a lineage member since her mother did not encourage her to enter into premarital relationships and to bear children. As Emilienne's elder sister had already given birth to several children from different relationships, her mother did not spend much effort encouraging Emilienne to do the same. Grandchildren are sought after but the number of grandchildren has to stay within the bounds of the possible. As Emilienne's mother already had to take care of many grandchildren, she did not prevent Emilienne from marriage, especially as she seemed to have a proper husband. When the marriage subsequently went wrong, Emilienne was given the daughter of her elder sister and her loneliness was compensated for. The way Emilienne's mother influenced Emilienne's trajectories and reinforced age hierarchies between siblings illustrates how important it is to focus not only on women's individual agency in matters of marriage, descent, and grandmotherhood but also on interdependent agency.

CONCLUSION

This article has argued that despite fluid generational demarcations between grandmothers and mothers, grandmotherhood in East Cameroon is differently perceived and performed from motherhood. Performances of grandmotherhood only partly confirm the results of comparative studies on relations between generations in West and East Africa, which generally suggest that in West Africa people do not sharply distinguish between parents and grandparents (Sangree 1974; Ruel 2002). In East Cameroon, grandmothers can indeed easily replace mothers in such a way that their grandchildren consider them to be their 'real' mothers but grandmothers perform their grandmotherhood differently from their motherhood. The sharing of home, food and bed is central in the performance of grandmotherhood and expresses a relationship of solidarity, warmth, and intimacy that contrasts with hierarchical and detached relationships between mothers and children.

Johnson-Hanks' model of vital conjunctures (2002) has been used to illustrate that women's lives in East Cameroon are not organised in well-defined stages that apply similarly to all women. Being involved in a complex and dynamic kinship and marriage system, the major life events of mothers are rarely clear in direction nor do they have fixed boundaries. Women regularly reconsider, negotiate, change or discontinue their choices concerning marriage and kinship, and this often makes their life course change. In conformity with Johnson-Hanks (*op. cit.*) I have explained that grandmotherhood consists of multiple trajectories or paths that do not occur at the same time or in the same order.

Multiple paths of grandmotherhood have been considered from the perspective of differences within and between life courses. Differences within have been explained from both grandmothers' own position towards marriage and their children's position towards marriage. From these different positions grandmothers have different relationships with different categories of grandchildren: children of unmarried sons, married daughters, married sons, and unmarried daughters. However, descriptions of these different relationships have also shown that categorical boundaries are never fixed but fluid and flexible since negotiations on rights in children continue throughout life and may change grandmothers' relationships with their grandchildren.

Though differences between grandmothers may well reflect differences within individual life courses, a focus on these differences draws attention to the interdependence of agency within the domains of marriage and descent. This interdependent agency has to be considered to capture women's multiple and flexible paths of grandmotherhood. Besides the agency of the intervening generation, age hierarchies between siblings and decisions of grandmothers' mothers also have an effect on grandmother–grandchild relationships.

In spite of these constraints, the article has aimed to explain that there certainly is room for individual agency. Grandmotherhood does not happen to mothers when their first grandchild is born, but it is actively chosen and enacted from the moment that women no longer enter into sexual and reproductive relationships with men. Then, women can claim a grandchild to share home, food, and bed and to enjoy their grandmotherhood. Even before claiming a grandchild and an intensive relationship of sharing becomes possible, women prepare future grandmotherhood when daughters are pregnant and deliver, when their grandchildren are being weaned, and through periodic visits of grandchildren. All the different aspects of grandmotherhood have illustrated that in this area, matrilineages and patrilineages are closely linked to each other.

Grandmothers' refraining from sexuality enables them to dedicate their time and energy to matters of descent. A point of discussion has been that grandmothers have hardly been taken seriously in anthropological theories of descent whereas grandmothers in East Cameroon strongly influence matrilineal affiliation in different ways. First, grandmothers are more powerful in claiming rights in children through signing birth certificates than biological fathers are. Second, the contributions of food and time that grandmothers make to the birth and growth of grandchildren have high value in the local kinship ideology. As grandmothers play central roles in negotiating matters of descent and make important interventions in the marriage and descent system, their relationships with grandchildren can be seen as one of the most important in society.

REFERENCES

Bledsoe, C. 2002. *Contingent Lives: fertility, time, and aging in West Africa*. Chicago: University of Chicago Press.

Bouquet, M. 1993. *Reclaiming English Kinship: Portuguese refractions of British kinship theory*. Manchester and New York: Manchester University Press.

Bourdieu, P. 1977. *Outline of a Theory of Practice*. Trans. by R. Nice. Cambridge: Cambridge University Press. (1972. *Esquisse d'une théorie de la pratique, précédé de trois études d'ethnologie kabyle*. Genève: Librairie Droz.).

Carsten, J. (ed.). 2000. *Cultures of Relatedness: new approaches to the study of kinship*. Cambridge: Cambridge University Press.

Copet, E. (Elisabeth Copet-Rougier). 1977. 'Nguélébok. Essai d'analyse de l'organisation sociale des Mkao Mbogendi'. Doctoral thesis. Paris: Université Paris 10.

Copet-Rougier, E. 1985. 'Contrôle masculin, exclusivité féminine dans une société patrilinéaire', in J.-C. Barbier (ed.), *Femmes du Cameroun: mères pacifiques, femmes rebelles*. Bondy: Orstom; Paris: Karthala.

——1987. ' "L'antilope accouche toujours de l'éléphant" (devinette Mkako): étude de la transformation du mariage chez les Mkako du Cameroun', in D. Parkin and D. Nyamwaya (eds), *Transformations of African Marriage*. Manchester and Wolfeboro NH: Manchester University Press, for the International African Institute.

Feldman-Savelsberg, P. 1996. 'Cooking inside: kinship and gender in Bangangté idioms of marriage and procreation', in M. J. Maynes, *et al.* (eds), *Gender, Kinship, Power: a comparative and interdisciplinary history*. New York and London: Routledge.

Gausset, Q. 1998. 'Double unilineal descent and triple kinship terminology: the case of the Kwanja of Cameroon', *Journal of the Royal Anthropological Institution* 4: 309–23.

Guyer, J. 1994. 'Lineal identities and lateral networks: the logic of polyandrous motherhood', in C. Bledsoe and G. Pison (eds), *Nuptiality in Sub-Saharan Africa: comtemporary anthropological and demographic perspectives*. Oxford: Clarendon Press.

Holy, L. 1996. *Anthropological Perspectives on Kinship*. London and Chicago: Pluto Press.

Johnson-Hanks, J. 2002. 'On the limits of life stages in ethnography: toward a theory of vital conjunctures', *American Anthropologist* 104: 865–80.

Karanja, W. W. 1987. ' "Outside wives" and "inside wives" in Nigeria: a study of changing perceptions in marriage', in D. Parkin and D. Nyamwaya (eds), *Transformations of African Marriage*. Manchester and Wolfeboro NH: Manchester University Press, for the International African Institute.

——1994. 'The phenomenon of "outside wives": some reflections on its possible influence on fertility', in C. Bledsoe and G. Pison (eds), *Nuptiality in Sub-Saharan Africa: comtemporary anthropological and demographic perspectives*. Oxford: Clarendon Press.

Maher, V. (ed.). 1995. *The Anthropology of Breast-feeding: natural law or social construct*. Oxford and Washington DC: Berg.

Mann, K. 1994. 'The historical roots and cultural logic of outside marriage in colonial Lagos', in C. Bledsoe and G. Pison (eds), *Nuptiality in Sub-Saharan Africa: comtemporary anthropological and demographic perspectives*. Oxford: Clarendon Press.

Moore, H. L. 1993. 'The differences within and the differences between', in T. del Valle (ed.), *Gendered Anthropology*. London: Routledge.

——1994. *A Passion for Difference: essays in anthropology and gender*. Cambridge: Polity Press.

Notermans, C. 1999. ' "Wanja, daar kun je er één, twee, zelfs drie van hebben": vrouwen met meer mannen in polygyne samenlevingen', *Tijdschrift voor Genderstudies* 2: 46–54.

——2003. 'Nomads in kinship: selves and fosterage in Cameroon', *Focaal: European Journal of Anthropology*.

Parkin, R. 1997. *Kinship: an introduction to the basic concepts*. Oxford: Blackwell Publishers.

Piot, C. 1999. *Remotely Global: village modernity in West Africa*. Chicago: University of Chicago Press.

Riesman, P. 1986. 'The person and the life cycle in African social life and thought', *African Studies Review* 29 (2): 71–138.

Ruel, M. 2002. 'The structural articulation of generations in Africa', *Cahier d'Études Africaines* 165: 51–81.

Sangree, W. 1974. 'Youth as elders and infants as ancestors: the complementarity of alternate generations, both living and dead, in Tiriki, Kenya, and Irigwe, Nigeria', *Africa* 44 (1): 65–70.

Schneider, D. 1984. *A Critique of the Study of Kinship*. Ann Arbor: The University of Michigan Press.

Schweitzer, P. P. (ed.). 2000. *Dividends of Kinship: meanings and uses of social relatedness*. London and New York: Routledge.

Stone, L. (ed.). 2000. *New Directions in Anthropological Kinship*. Lanham MD and Oxford: Rowman & Littlefield.

Woodburn, J. 1998. ' "Sharing is not a form of exchange": an analysis of property-sharing in immediate-return hunter-gatherer societies', in C. M. Hann (ed.), *Property Relations: renewing the anthropological tradition*. Cambridge: Cambridge University Press.

ABSTRACT

This article focuses on relationships between grandmothers and grandchildren in an urban society in East Cameroon. It argues that despite fluid generational demarcations between grandmothers and mothers, women perform their grandmotherhood differently from their motherhood. As a result of the claims grandmothers often make on their children's children, grandmothers easily replace mothers but they do not rear children in the same way. The sharing of home, food, and bed is central in the performance of grandmotherhood and differs from relationships of sharing in the mother–child bond. The article also argues that grandmotherhood in East Cameroon is not a clearly bounded, unambiguous life stage but that it contains multiple trajectories that do not occur in the same time or in the same order. Multiple trajectories, characterised by both agency and constraint, are explained in terms of differences within and between grandmothers' life courses. The article shows that grandmothers play vital roles in complex practices of marriage and descent and, in contrast to previous studies in the area, that matrilineages are closely linked to patrilineages.

RÉSUMÉ

Cet article s'intéresse aux relations entre les grands-mères et leurs petits-enfants dans une société urbaine du Cameroun oriental. Il montre qu'en dépit de démarcations générationnelles fluides entre les grands-mères et les mères, les femmes exercent leur grand-maternité différemment de leur maternité. En conséquence des droits que les grands-mères revendiquent souvent sur les enfants de leurs enfants, les grands-mères remplacent facilement les mères mais ne les élèvent pas de la même manière. Le partage du domicile, de la nourriture et du lit est un élément essentiel de la grand-maternité et diffère des relations de partage qui s'exercent dans le lien mère-enfant. L'article montre également qu'au Cameroun oriental la grand-maternité n'est pas une étape de vie clairement délimitée et sans équivoque, mais contient des trajectoires multiples qui ne surviennent pas au même moment ni dans le même ordre. Ces trajectoires multiples, caractérisées à la fois par l'action et la contrainte, sont expliquées en termes de différences entre les parcours de vie des grands-mères et au sein de ces parcours. L'article montre que les grands-mères jouent des rôles essentiels dans les pratiques complexes du mariage et de la descendance et, par contraste avec les études précédentes dans ce domaine, que les matrilignages sont étroitement liés aux patrilignages.

GRANDPARENTS AS FOSTER-PARENTS: TRANSFORMATIONS IN FOSTER RELATIONS BETWEEN GRANDPARENTS AND GRANDCHILDREN IN NORTHERN BENIN

In memory of Bona Taowere (*c.*1910–2000)

Erdmute Alber

Bona Taowere was an old woman in the Baatombu village of Tɛbɔ where I have been doing research since 1992. She called me her granddaughter, and in our many conversations over the years she told me about her life and tried to bring me closer to an understanding of her view of the world. The first time we met, she was full of resentment as she told me the story of an unsuccessful attempt to take on a grandchild as a foster-child. Shortly after Dahomey gained independence (later to become the Republic of Benin), she went to her nephew Sacca, a civil servant who worked in the Benin capital, Cotonou, and asked him to give her his daughter. But Sacca refused her request. Bona told me this story again and again until her death in 2000. Although the event had taken place many years ago, she could not forget it and did not stop talking about it. She experienced this event as a profound insult and a rejection. It gave her the impression that fundamental norms she had grown up with were changing. She often spoke about this as well. When I met Sacca in 1999 he was retired and living in Cotonou.[1] He could hardly remember the incident that Bona had so often described to me. He knew Bona, of course, as she was known far beyond Tɛbɔ, but the incident seemed to be less present to him than to her. In response to my inquiry, he noted that in the past years he had so many requests for his children that he could not remember them all any more. He had, of course, always refused such requests.

This text is about a particular constellation of grandparents and grandchildren that is widespread but on the decline among the Baatombu in northern Benin: the fostering of children by their classificatory grandparents. Among the Baatombu, it is common for classificatory grandparents to become foster-parents to their grandchildren, being granted the full rights, as well as the responsibilities and financial obligations, of parents. Not only do they feed, clothe and raise their grandchildren, but also find them a husband or wife and

---

ERDMUTE ALBER is Junior Professor of Social Anthropology at the University of Bayreuth. An account of her research on the transformation of power among the Baatombu in northern Benin, *Im Gewand von Herrschaft. Modalitäten der Macht bei den Baatombu (1895–1995)*, was published by Rüdiger Köppe Verlag, Köln, in 2000. More recently she has been researching into kinship and family changes in West Africa.

[1] Sacca died in Cotonou in 2001 at the age of seventy and was buried in his hometown of Wenou, about fifty kilometres from Tɛbɔ. He belonged to the generation of urban Baatombu in Benin who had been born in the villages and who identified very strongly with their villages for the rest of their lives. The old village traditions and norms had remained present in his family more than in other urban Baatombu families.

pay for their wedding. Fostering means that the grandparents take on the position of parents and thereby give up some of the specific roles of grandparents. Not only do they enjoy the daily presence of their grandchildren, they also gain a parent's rights to the labour power of the children, which serves as a substantial contribution to their social security in old age. The fostering of grandchildren by their grandparents among the Baatombu is part of a general practice of child-fostering. Until a few years ago, the majority of Baatombu children grew up not with their biological parents but with relatives (Alber 2003). I will start with a general description of kinship relations among the Baatombu and some comments on the ways kinship, fosterage and grandparenthood are discussed in the literature about West Africa. From there I will address the phenomenon of social parenting. Having set up this background, I will consider the relationship between grandparents and grandchildren. Finally, I will address social change pertaining to child-fostering and the question of why these changes particularly affect the elderly.

KINSHIP AMONG THE BAATOMBU AND IN WEST AFRICA

The circa 600,000 Baatombu belong to the Gur-speaking ethnic groups in the West African savannah. Their area of settlement is called Borgu, a bush savannah extending to the river Niger in the East and to the Atacora mountains on the Benin–Togo frontier in the West. Since the beginning of the twentieth century, precolonial Borgu has been divided by the international frontier between Benin and Nigeria.[2] They are farmers who share the Benin areas of Borgu with the cattle rearing Fulɓe and other farming groups such as the Boko and Mokolle, as well as with the growing multiethnic urban population in which different peoples from all over Benin are represented.

The kinship system of the Baatombu is very similar to that of the Tallensi, which has been described in the classic study by Meyer Fortes (1949) as typical for the different Gur-speaking groups. It is characterised by patrilineal descent and an underlying clan system. Living arrangements follow the rule of patrivirilocality: men remain on their father's homestead after they marry, unless they establish their own homestead. Married women live with their husbands, but they may return to their own family's homestead in old age. Thus homesteads are generally inhabited by the male descendants of the founder of a homestead, that is, fathers, sons, grandchildren and their brothers. In addition, the wives of these men and their unmarried or no longer married sisters and daughters live with them. Also inhabiting

---

[2] In the English and French ethnological literature, the Baatombu are often called Bariba—see, for example, Lombard (1965). I prefer to use the term they themselves use. On the Baatombu and Borgu in general, see Alber (2000), Crowder (1983), Kuba (1996), Lombard (1965), and Sargent (1988). This account is based exclusively on research among the Baatombu in Benin.

the homestead are men and women of all ages who were once taken in as foster-children, unmarried children and youths who still have the status of foster-children, or married men who came to the homestead as foster-children and stayed there as adults. And former foster-children who are now married have their wives, children and foster-children with them at the homestead.

Meyer Fortes' central thesis concerning kinship among the Tallensi, which has been applied to the savannah groups in general, is that despite patrilinearity and patrilocality, the family of the mother has a very important role for individuals. Not only do the maternal kin represent potential support during times of crisis or when applying for office; certain persons such as the maternal uncles have extensive rights to their sisters' children and are connected to them through a joking relation.

Drawing on Meyer Fortes' work, other authors have addressed the issue of patrilinearity with strong ties to the maternal lineage. Often this is examined with the example of the special position of the mother's brother. Jack Goody (1959: 81) has formulated the problem as a 'basic contradiction between the principle of unilineal descent and the unity of the sibling group. For unilineal descent splits the sibling group into the sibling relevant for reckoning of descent and the residual sibling who cannot transmit membership to his or her offspring.' He thereby relegates the position of maternal kin to the status of 'residual' kin and attributes to them a subordinate role in relation to the patrilineage. In other descriptions, for example in Gottlieb's work (1992) on the Beng in Sierra Leone, more emphasis is placed on the complementary relationship between the two descendant groups forming the basis of a system of thought consisting of two complementary types of social relations (*op. cit.*: 49).

Other authors have since shown that Meyer Fortes overlooked or at least underestimated certain institutions in the kinship system. Barbara Meier's research (1993, 1999) for example, has shown that the foster-parenting of nieces among the Bulsa allows not only the mother's brother but also the father's sister certain rights to the children of their siblings. The paternal aunt takes on a special responsibility for the life of the child and is responsible also for carrying out the life-granting birth ritual; but, in addition, she also has the right to take on her niece as a foster-child and to later give her away in marriage. In the institution of niece-fostering, according to Meier, the important role of women as sisters and aunts becomes apparent—a role that has been overlooked by most authors. While the conventional ethnological view saw women as wives and mothers and thus addressed their position only within the homestead of their husbands, in their roles as sisters and aunts women are active and powerful within their own kinship group. Their position there is much stronger than in the context of their husband's family.

Looking at the foster relations between grandparents and grandchildren among the Baatombu offers an example very similar to Meier's to complement the image of kinship relations sketched by Meyer Fortes for the West African savannah. An important lesson of the Baatombu example is that women should not be understood only in the roles of mothers, wives, aunts and sisters, as Meier insists, but also as grandmothers who can take on foster-children and, thus engage in a 'politics of fostering'. This role is predicated upon exercising the role of mother and then the 'completion' of that role by giving away the daughter in marriage. Grandmothers receive grandchildren as gifts in return for the (biological or foster-) daughters they have given away into marriage.

According to Fortes, in general a trusting and often warm emotional relationship exists between grandparents and grandchildren, while the relationship of parents to children is characterised by authority. Remnants of the relationship of authority are found only between the paternal grandparents and their grandchildren because of the paternal grandfather's function as the head of the homestead. But the paternal grandparents leave punishment, should it be necessary, to the parents. The maternal grandparents, however, bear no traces of authority and strictness. Beyond the joking relation, the relationship between the maternal grandparents and their grandchildren is characterised exclusively by love and closeness, and nothing else is expected of this relationship.

Meyer Fortes mentions that 'children often sleep with a grandparent' and 'a woman whose father- or mother-in-law is alive always has someone with whom to leave her baby' (1949: 237). But he does not consider the question of the importance placed on foster relations between grandparents and grandchildren. In the West African Sudan, however, the temporary or permanent fostering of children by their grandparents is quite common. Bledsoe and Isingo-Abanike (1989) have shown the immense importance of fosterage in Sierra Leone as a form of support in old age, suggesting that by fostering grandchildren, grandmothers are able to assert their demands on their children. Esther Goody (1982: 159 ff.) also specifies grandparents among the Gonja as the second most important group of foster-parents after classificatory uncles and aunts. On the basis of these findings, I think that the question of fosterage and foster-parent roles has to be taken more into account in the discussion about grandparents in Africa.

FOSTER-PARENTING AMONG THE BAATOMBU: SOME STATISTICAL DATA

Among the Baatombu, the circulation of children through foster relations constitutes a central feature of the social organisation. It is commonly practised and not merely a phenomenon that arises in situations of crisis.[3] Unlike in other parts of Africa where AIDS

---

[3] On the meaning of child-fostering in West Africa as represented by the Gonja in Ghana, see above all Esther Goody (1982). Other case studies have been done by, among others, Allman (1997), Atto (1996), Bledsoe (1980), Bledsoe and Brandon (1992), Bledsoe and Isingo-Abanike (1989), Isaac *et al.* (1982), Lallemand (1993, 1994), Page (1989) and Roost Vischer (1997). The quantitative significance of the phenomenon is emphasised particularly by Page (1989).

orphans are often raised by their grandparents because their parents' generation is no longer present (see Benedicte Ingstadt's contribution in this volume), fosterage is exercised by the Baatombu as a means of strengthening and renewing social ties between kin. Until recent years, Baatombu children grew up with foster-parents more often than with their biological parents. Unsystematic surveys of older people I carried out in Baatombu villages showed that more than 90% of those over seventy years of age did not spend their childhood with their biological parents.

Based on this information, I organised systematic surveys in three Baatombu villages, Kika, Yaro and Tɛbɔ. In each of these villages at least sixty men and women over fifty years of age were surveyed about their own childhood and that of their children.[4] In Kika, 65% of those over fifty years of age had spent their childhood with foster-parents, in Yaro the figure was 43%, and in Tɛbɔ a total of 49%. In the generation of the children of the men and women surveyed,[5] foster-parenting had decreased significantly, although the figures were quite different in each of the villages. In Kika and Tɛbɔ, the figure was approximately 40%, while in Yaro only 14% of children of the younger generation had grown up with foster-parents. The data show the commonness of foster care, particularly for the older generation, and a remarkable decline in the younger generation. Depending on the region, however, even today between 10% and 40% of rural Baatombu children grow up with foster-parents, which is quite comparable with Page's data (1989) from Ghana and Sierra Leone.

There is a remarkable gender bias in foster practices which has apparently increased in the last decades. Taking the example of Kika, the figures are still balanced in the elder generation: 63% of the men and 67% of the women had experienced foster care, whereas in the younger

---

[4] The surveys in Kika and Yaro were carried out in March 2002, and in Tɛbɔ in November 2002. A twelve-page questionnaire on the course of their lives, family structure, children and other data was filled out for men and women over fifty years of age, the majority of whom were illiterate and all of whom were farmers. The questionnaire solicited information on various topics including the biological children of those surveyed, including age, sex, where they grew up, their education, etc. We also asked for information about children who had died and about foster-children. The total number of children of the 186 Baatombu surveyed in the three villages was as follows: 361 in Kika, 547 in Yaro, and 499 in Tɛbɔ. This yields an average birth rate of 7.6 per surveyed adult. We were careful to survey the same number of men as women. Conversation was in the Baatonum language. I thank Anna Jahn, Regina Sarreiter, Saliou Agani and Adjara Alou for their help with the surveys.

[5] I use the concept of generations here not in the sociological sense of Karl Mannheim (1928), who associates it with certain communalities among an age cohort, but rather as a concept of family relations. It was more appropriate in this case to research the changes in child-fostering not just among people of different ages to see if the rate of fostering changed with the younger ones, but also to survey a certain group of people and then to ask for information about their children and thus about the following generation. The systematic difference is that the generation of children in the survey is very heterogeneous in terms of age (from infants to forty-year-olds), yet whole groups of siblings were taken into account whose ages are sometimes quite different.

generation only 33 % of the boys but 48% of the girls grew up as foster-children. In other villages, already in the elder generation a gender difference was found, which increased in the younger generation. The most extreme case is the village of Tɛbɔ, where in the young generation 63% of the women grew up as foster-girls, but only 17% of the men. Comparing the two generations, foster care had even increased in the case of the women, whereas it had decreased for both women and men in the other investigated villages.[6]

My conversations with people over seventy years of age who had almost exclusively grown up in foster care lead to the conclusion that before the colonisation of Borgu in the last decade of the nineteenth century and before the general decline in foster care set in, there had been no or only a slight difference between the genders concerning the question of foster care; almost all children, boys as well as girls, grew up as foster-children. Colonial and post-colonial influences led to the changes mentioned here, and in particular to the gender differences. Foster care has increasingly become a phenomenon that affects girls.

However, the most important result of the survey for the theme of this article is the important role of grandparents as foster-parents of their grandchildren. A third of all foster-children—be it in the elder or in the younger generation—grew up with grandparents. After the aunts and uncles, who take about 60% of the children being fostered out, the grandparents are the second largest group of foster-parents. There is no remarkable change between the generations in this aspect. Only a small minority of about 10% of the children in all three villages and in both generations were fostered by other kin.

A differentiated look at the general categories of 'grandparents' and 'aunts and uncles' also shows that not all individuals within these categories are as likely to foster children. Most children who are fostered by someone belonging to the category 'aunts and uncles' are in fact fostered by their paternal aunt. Among grandparents, it is grandmothers, and especially maternal grandmothers, who foster. To finish summarising the results of the quantitative data, there is another important gender aspect in foster practices: girls were and are almost always fostered by women, and boys by men. Thus, the data show

---

[6] I will not address the particularities of each of the three villages in this text. But the following should be mentioned: Yaro is the most dynamic in terms of its development; it is involved in more village development projects; it has the oldest school; in agricultural terms it is technologically the most advanced; and the Christian mission there has had a greater influence than in Kika or Tɛbɔ. The steep decline in child-fostering may correspond to the modernity of the village. Kika and Tɛbɔ are more traditional villages with fewer indications of development. But as explicated in Alber (2000), Tɛbɔ is distinguished by the fact that in earlier times it was an important village and the centre of a *canton* with contact to the French colonial administration, though it has become less important since the 1930s. The data correspond to this description in so far as Tɛbɔ can be understood as a more 'modern' village with a lower rate of child-fostering, similar to Yaro. But it later lost some of its modernity and the figures for the younger generations are closer to those in Kika, where fostering had been continued as a tradition.

that the fosterage of girls seems to be an affair of women, whereas the fosterage of boys is an affair of men.

NORMS AND PRACTICES OF FOSTER-PARENTING

Given these statistical data, I shall now consider how they fit with the norms and rules people mention when talking about fosterage. Firstly, foster-parenting is based on the idea that children do not belong solely to their parents and that the parents cannot claim them as their own. As mentioned above, the farm homesteads consist of the fathers, sons, cousins and brothers of a patriclan, who live together with their wives, children, and foster-children, and who produce the food for their homestead together. Women come into these families after a bride price has been paid for them and certain bride services have been carried out. For several years in advance of a marriage, the family of the bride receives certain gifts that are seen as compensation for the anticipated fertility of the bride, that is, for the children the woman will bear and who will become members of the patriclan.[7] The payment of the bride price thus starts building up a network of circulations of goods and persons between the two families, the fosterage of children being one component of it.

The bride price has to be reciprocated by the family of the wife with smaller gifts. The wedding follows, in which the woman is given by her family to the family of her husband and which is accompanied by an abundant circulation of various goods and food in both directions. The marriage of a woman is above all tied to the expectation that she will bear children for the family of her husband. Other gifts are given by the family of the husband to that of the wife following the wedding and continuing as long as the woman bears children. In addition, there is also the circulation of children as foster-children, which follows the ideal pattern as mapped out below.

When a woman is about to give birth to a first child, she usually returns to her parents' homestead for the birth, remaining there for up to two years until the child is weaned and the woman is ready to become pregnant again. Shortly after the birth, her husband's family sends her certain gifts, and the husband comes to the homestead of his wife's family to visit her and to pay his respects to the family. The paternal aunt plays a key role in the birth of a first child. As a female representative of the husband's clan, and thus the clan of the new child, she visits the new mother and her family, distributes ritual gifts to the mother and declares that the child is a member of the husband's patriclan. As with all gifts circulated between the families of a married couple, these gifts are reciprocated.

---

[7] Caroline Bledsoe (2002) has emphasised in a very differentiated way the importance of fertility for the women themselves and for their own families. On the importance of fertility for Baatombu women, see also Sargent (1982).

The child is then considered the property of this paternal aunt, who has the right to foster it. If she does not want the child, she can give it to another person in the paternal family, or someone else from the paternal family can claim it as their own. With the birth of a first child, the marriage is consummated, and at the same time the ritual gift-giving to the mother documents the final step in the transition of a young girl into a married woman and mother.

The circulation of gifts and persons between the husband's family and that of the wife does not end here; it is continued with the birth of the second child. Here, at the latest, and if the first child was taken by the aunt, the grandmother starts to have a role in the circulation system. The second child is understood as a reciprocal gift to the social mother of the woman giving birth to the children, that is, to whoever had raised her and given her away in marriage. Many of those whom I spoke with emphasised the reciprocal character of the second birth. When the daughter left her mother as a girl to become a woman, the mother lost her daughter's labour power as well as the closeness with her, giving these to the future husband. Therefore, she is entitled to the second child resulting from the marriage of her daughter and her son-in-law.

The couple's additional children also circulate in both the paternal and maternal family, and to the classificatory siblings of the parents of the child—aunts and uncles—as well as to the classificatory grandparents. In all cases, if the parents' siblings take the children, the transfer is accompanied by gifts to the child's mother; whereas grandparents do not give anything for 'their' child.

But the circle of those involved in these transactions is less well defined and in part dependent upon the gender of the first two children. If they were both boys, then the maternal grandmother can claim the third child as her own. If the second child circulated in the family of its mother, the paternal family can also lay claim to the third child. The fourth child is considered to belong to the parents themselves, given that the first three children did not die as infants and were thus able to be given away.

The explicitly reciprocal character of giving the second child to the mother's mother seems to me to explain to some extent why some kinds of fosterage are not tied to the exchange of gifts and others are. Aunts and uncles, especially those of the father's clan, combine the fostering of a child with gift-giving to the mother. In the case of the siblings of the child's father, this can be understood as reciprocation for the reproductive work of the woman, i.e. for her having given a child to the husband's family. But even the mother's siblings give something, although less formal and ritual, to the mother of a child if they claim it officially. This is seen as a sign of gratitude for getting a child. However, grandparents fostering a child never give anything to the mother—they simply claim the child as their own. In the case of the maternal grandmother this is evident: she is not responsible for reciprocating because she has not just received but already given something, namely, her own daughter. Furthermore, the generation of the grandparents is seen in general as having the right to get 'their' children without having to reciprocate: having already given birth to the parents' generation, they possess the full rights of claiming whomever they want to raise among the grandchildren.[8]

Put in a formal way, the children given to classificatory siblings of the father can be considered a gift which is reciprocated with gifts to the child's mother, while children given to the maternal grandmother are the reciprocation for her own child whom she gave away in marriage. And, furthermore, having given birth to children, the grandparent's generation has the right to receive the gifts of the grandparents without being obliged to reciprocate this act with other gifts.

Amidst all these rules—and we see that in practice the rules are flexible—what is important is that those who foster children *ask* for them, and that according to official practice a child may not be 'offered' by its parents. The parents' role can rather be described as not rejecting requests for their children. According to the old viewpoint, which is gradually changing now, they did not have the right to refuse requests. The persons who request children are always ones whose standing in the family hierarchy is higher than that of the child's parents. Younger siblings do not have the right to request a child.

IDEALS VERSUS REALITY IN FOSTER-PARENTING

The statistics confirm the ideals of fostering practices as mapped out above to the extent that in fact many children do still grow up today as foster-children. They also confirm the special roles of the paternal aunt and the maternal grandmother. But as has been shown, the quantitative data also confirm that the number of children being given away today is steadily declining.

The data show additionally that with each new birth within a marriage, the likelihood of the child being given as a foster-child decreases. First born children are most often given away; boys are the least likely to be given away. This is mostly related to the fact that the more children the parents bear and the older they become relatively in the kinship system, the easier it is for them to oppose requests for their children. For young parents, on the other hand, it is particularly difficult to refuse requests, as I was often told in discussions.

The way the ideal practices of foster care are lived out in Baatombu villages is more flexible and varied than the rules suggest. For example, divorce, which is common, plays a large role. In advance of a decision to divorce, many women try to give away children to their own family by secretly asking relatives to request a child. In this way they make leaving their husband's homestead easier and they secure further contact with and influence over their children.

---

[8] A very similar argument is mentioned in Noterman's article in this volume.

Other influences on the practices of fosterage are changes in norms. A European family image, in which children belong above all to their parents, has not only been disseminated by churches and missionaries during the colonial period but also written into national law, and the younger generation's reception of it is increasingly positive. Today many parents try to oppose giving up their children to foster-parents. They oppose fostering more often with boys because boys likelier go to school than girls, and because in general more value is placed on the education of boys than of girls. Rural foster-parents are often suspected of first assuring that their own children receive schooling before foster-children are sent to school. Thus parents try to prevent their children from being given away if they wish for them to go to school. Many parents think that it is particularly unlikely that grandparents will send their foster-children to school. This is the main reason for them to prevent the fostering of their children by the grandparents. But at the same time, opposing fostering by the grandparents is considered particularly problematic because grandparents should be granted even more respect than older siblings.

There is another reason why the foster care of girls persists more than that of boys. Fostering her sister's or brother's daughter gives a woman the right to foster, later on, the daughter of her foster-child, and, thus, to become a grandmother with foster-children. As described above, women can acquire power in their own family by fostering children, which strengthens their position in the homestead. In general, men complain more about the burdens of fostering children. They have to cover the costs of feeding and educating the children, and they often complain that it brings them little, particularly because today many boys leave their foster-parents as youths. Women, however, meaning both aunts and grandmothers, always emphasise the gains for them in fostering children. The child helps and supports them in their work, and they have the company of their own family members at their husband's homestead. And they do not feel as threatened as the men by the idea of the girls leaving as youths because girls in the villages are usually married shortly after they reach maturity and thus it is expected that they will leave their foster-mother at an early age.

The girls' marriages will also bring new privileges and opportunities for them. The marriage of a daughter secures for the social mother a new relationship with the husband's family which commits them to provide reciprocal gifts and services for years to come. And finally, by giving away a girl in marriage, a foster-mother has the option of fostering one of the bride's children and thus becoming a social mother again as a grandmother.

An important change in norms is that the urban population no longer send their children to foster care in the villages. This was, for example, the reason why Bona Taowere's request to foster (with which this article began) was rejected. Urban life is seen by both urban dwellers and by the rural population as very different from life in the villages. Above all, urban life is associated with different opportunities. The behaviour of urban children is considered to be different, and it is assumed that they will go to school. According to popular opinion, if urban children are put in foster care in the countryside, they will not be offered the same lifestyle as their urban siblings and they will be raised with different norms.

Villagers no longer even ask for urban children. But on the other hand, many children from the villages are sent to the cities and towns, sometimes only temporarily, in order to attend school there or as foster-children whose foster-parents are willing to take over the responsibility of feeding and educating them. The foster-children participate in the domestic work of the urban households.

The unidirectional exchange of children between rural and urban households has become very common. This started already in the late colonial period when the very rare Baatombu families in Cotonou or other large cities of the country housed nearly all the young Baatombu men who attended secondary schools or universities. This was not possible in the Baatombu villages and was even rare in Borgu in general with the exception of its capital, Parakou. Even today nearly every urban Baatombu civil servant or graduate in Benin older than forty years has experienced fosterage.[9] Due to the unidirectionality of the exchange of children today, people of the younger generation of Baatombu in the urban places—the children of the civil servants or graduates who came to the cities as foster-children—are the first Baatombu lacking systematic foster experience.

TASKS OF FOSTER-CHILDREN AND CHANGING OPINIONS ABOUT THE FOSTERAGE OF GRANDCHILDREN

In the Baatombu villages, however, even today, most of the old people, especially women, are surrounded by foster-children. When I did my interviews with old women like Bona Taowere, there was almost always a little girl around, lying down on the mat of her grandmother, listening to our conversations and being frequently sent out to fetch water or a dish for me. In the cases of the old men, foster-children are not as common but still frequent. Foster-boys accompany their grandfathers and help them in their everyday activities, such as doing little handicrafts, walking to the fields or gathering herbs from the bush. If grandparents become disabled or lose their sight, as happens frequently in Baatombu villages where medical service is still rare, foster-children help them to walk around, to find things in the house or to wash themselves. If grandfathers are still able to move around alone, but are too old to work in the fields, their foster-sons are usually integrated into the everyday labour in the fields. Girls fostered by their grandmothers help as well in the everyday activities of women like fetching water and wood, cooking, washing dishes and so on. Thus, the fosterage of children by grandparents does not primarily help to guarantee provision of the elder generation with

---

[9] The only exceptions are those Baatombu who grew up in boarding schools of missionaries or the state.

food—this is the task of the adults in the households, and specially the task of the head of the family. Rather, the task of the foster-children is to care for the grandparents and to help them in their everyday activities.

The frequent fostering of Baatombu children by classificatory grandparents is part of a general practice of social parenting and cannot be understood outside of this context. Giving children to grandparents is a constituent part of a complex process of exchange that is essential to kinship relations among the Baatombu. These exchange relations have a horizontal and a vertical plane. On the horizontal plane, marriage binds together two families and creates affinal kinship relations which are confirmed and built upon through foster care and the exchange of gifts. Vertical relations, on the other hand, refer to the exchange relations that occur between different generations. Parents give their children away in marriage and receive grandchildren as foster-children, whom they can also give away in marriage and thereby gain the rights to new foster-children.

In recent decades, however, not only are foster relations in general changing but also the relationship between grandparents and grandchildren. Of the generations involved in fosterage, the grandparents are the ones who view its decline most negatively; they see themselves as losing out. The middle generations and the children themselves are ambivalent about the decline of fosterage in general, and often they even see the change as positive. Children who experienced foster-parenting complain about having been disadvantaged in comparison with children who grew up with their biological parents—for example, that they were not allowed to go to school, or that they were treated poorly by their foster-parents.

The middle generation is the most ambivalent in their attitude toward fostering. Many parents would like to keep their biological children, but they complain that they are not always able to assert themselves on this matter. Many men complain that the investments made in the costs of keeping foster-children are not worth it if the children leave as youths. My overall impression was that many people in the middle generation try to keep as many of their biological children as possible without risking major conflicts with their relatives. But at the same time, they are open to fostering the children of others.

The older generation, however, does not want to give up the practice of grandparental fosterage, and they complain loudly that this tradition is increasingly less recognised. Because their children are already grown, they will not benefit from the changes that make it easier for biological parents to keep their children. Within the parameters of the old norms, they have made their contributions to the system of circulation: they gave up many of their children to fosterage, and they gave those they raised away in marriage. For them, the decline in fosterage means nothing but a loss; they receive nothing, or at least less, from the system of circulation.

In discussions with older people, stories of past rejection in requests for foster-parenting often come up, much like the example of Bona Taowere described above. From the perspective of the older generation, this rejection is an affront to established hierarchies, an expression of dwindling respect for the elders, and ultimately evidence that the rules with which they were brought up are no longer valid today. In addition, they are worried about who will help the elderly in their everyday life in the future.

But fosterage and in particular the practice of having children grow up among older people is not completely shunned by younger generations. In general many Baatombu believe that it is good for children to be raised by people other than their biological parents. It is said that parents are not strict enough with their children, while foster-parents can better teach them to obey their elders—an important criterion in child rearing—as well as correct behaviour and the ability to withstand difficult situations.

DIFFERENT VERSIONS OF GRANDPARENTHOOD

Interestingly, grandparents are not usually associated with this ideal image of childrearing. Outside the institution of child fosterage, the relationship between grandparents and grandchildren, just as Meyer Fortes had described, is considered affectionate and close. Grandparents and grandchildren, if not bound together by a foster relation, are also seen as 'equal', that is, the relationship is understood as negating the authority differential created by the social hierarchy based on age.

The notion of the equality between alternating generations is also manifest in the traditional alternation of two different generation names which are part of everyone's name. The generational names are *wure* and *kpai*. The son of a *wure* is a *kpai*, and the *kpai*'s son, i.e. the *wure*'s grandson, is also a *wure*. While the adjacent generations are said to be very different from each other, grandparents and grandchildren are considered to be similar and equal.

The equality between grandparents and grandchildren is expressed in daily life through their joking relations. Grandparents, both paternal and maternal, call their grandchildren husband or wife, and the grandchildren return this jest with coquettish behaviour and sexual innuendo that is unusual even for married couples in public. This has often been described. This presumed similarity and lack of hierarchy between alternating generations, however, prevents one type of child-fostering, namely the fostering of great-grandchildren. Unlike parents, who claim the right to the children of their children and take them in as foster-children, on principle grandparents do not ask their grandchildren for their children.

The reason why it is not possible to ask a grandchild to give up his or her children for fostering is that the hierarchy and inequality necessary to the relationship in which a child is requested is missing in the relationship between grandparents and their grandchildren. The request, or demand, for the rights to a child, as mentioned above, is in principle associated with a hierarchical differential between the foster-parents and the biological parents. For this reason, it is older siblings who ask for the children of their younger siblings, and these younger siblings may make such demands only on their younger classificatory siblings. Hierarchy is also inherent to the relationship between classificatory parents and children, the other relationship in which demands for children are made. Grandparents, on the other hand, cannot make such demands on their grandchildren because, in the joking relation, they are considered to be their marital spouses and thus their equals, such that the necessary authority for such demands is missing.

The only exception to this norm is the fostering of a great-grandchild by an old woman if the child's mother is her foster-child. If this is the case, the grandmother is understood first and foremost as a social mother and thus as an authority figure, which creates enough of a hierarchical differential that she has a clear claim to the second daughter as reciprocation. In this case her role as a grandmother, that is, as an 'equal', does not take precedence.

This case makes reference to a general difference between the relationships of grandparents and grandchildren related by fosterage and those who are 'only' related by grandparenthood. The joking relation and feigned equality give way, in the second case, to the respect and obedience typical for the interaction between parents and children among the Baatombu. In a foster relation, grandparents take the role of authority figures, typical for the parent–child relation, making a joking relation impossible. Their task becomes much more to teach the child and to guarantee a strict and adequate education than to play with the child. I have occasionally observed how strict a woman is with her granddaughter whom she has taken in as a foster-child and how the girl is made to do work, while at the same time she jokingly demonstrates intimacy with the girl's younger brother who is visiting, giving him delicacies to snack on and explaining that she must prepare a good meal for her 'husband'.

Foster-parents are generally expected to teach their children everything they will need to know in later life. Caroline Bledsoe (1990) has observed that in Sierra Leone the harsh and strict treatment of foster-children is justified by the saying 'no success without struggle' and that in general it is assumed that a strict upbringing will benefit children as adults. This is also true in the case of the Baatombu. Harsh and strict treatment of fostered grandchildren—that is, more 'parental' than 'grandparental'—is generally accepted and is seen as part of a normal upbringing. The memories of adults who spent their childhood as foster-children of their grandparents, however, vary from scenes of harshness and strictness to friendly devotion and pampering.

There are some adults who remember a childhood as 'spoiled children' (*bii kɔsa*), having had too much love and care from different persons. These are mostly those who grew up as foster-children in the homestead of their biological parents. Being a foster-child does not always mean having grown up completely separated from one's biological parents; for example, a person may be fostered by a grandmother or grandfather living in the same homestead as one's parents. Children growing up in this constellation have a good chance of being spoiled because they receive food and attention from their foster-parents as well as from their biological parents. This constellation seems to have guaranteed double the amount of food and other forms of material attention—and food connotes affection and care of all kinds in the memories of those I interviewed. It also meant a particularly comfortable climate for children. This suggests that the experience of separation from the biological mother as a child was not as easy as is often described in childhood memories.

GRANDPARENTS AS LOSERS IN THE TRANSFORMATIONS?

Comparing the statistical results with the statements of elder Baatombu, who claim they are losing out in the decline of foster-parenting, it seems initially that the figures contradict their statements. In terms of the percentage of fosterage overall, the proportion of grandparents who foster children has not decreased, and in some villages it has even increased. This has also been confirmed by the statements of younger people who are critical of the practice. They say it is particularly difficult to reject a grandparent's request for a child. Young parents often feel that they are not in a position to oppose these wishes, particularly because such wishes are backed with the power of norms that are still valid and only gradually are loosening up.

The statements of older people are not unfounded, however, because as foster-parenting has declined overall, the numbers of grandparents fostering grandchildren have also declined. In the village context today, remaining with the biological parents is no longer an exception associated with the rare but attractive image of a pampered child; it is now a second normal course of childhood among the Baatombu that exists parallel to child-fostering, which remains a widespread phenomenon. The older generation is affected by the decline of foster care in so far as they are not the protagonists of the changes, but instead must simply accept them as they gradually develop. The decline of child-fostering is at least partially advocated by the younger generations because it gives biological parents more freedom and autonomy in deciding where their children shall grow up.

The example of Bona Taowere described at the outset of this article refers beyond the local changes in norms and practices within the villages also to the larger issue of the transformation in relations between urban and rural life. In this respect as well, members of the older generation are not active protagonists but are affected by the change.[10] Borgu

---

[10] I explicitly prefer to use the expression that someone is not a protagonist of change to the widely used expression of being a 'victim' of change, because the latter presupposes a lack of possible responses to, and even a passive acceptance of, change. The grandparent generation is actively participating in these events and trying to assert their own interests. It is not without reason that so many of those I spoke with told me how hard it is to turn down the request of grandparents to foster children.

is a region with a high population growth rate which has increased the population density in rural areas and thereby led to a gradual scarcity of land as well as to increased migration. In the households of urban Baatombu in Cotonou and Parakou (the regional centre of Borgu) where I also carried out surveys on child-fostering, I found that surprisingly few people of the grandparent generation were living there. Most households were made up of two generations consisting of parents and children, plus foster-children and classificatory siblings of the parents. The parental generation consists primarily of men and women who were born in the villages and who moved to the towns as children or youths. Most of the grandparent generation, i.e. the parents of this migrant generation, still lived in the villages.

As described above, among the Baatombu, children of urban dwellers are no longer sent to the villages as foster-children. The circulation of children between the countryside and the towns has thus become unidirectional; the migration of youths from the villages generally occurs through foster relations in households in the towns, where they are taken in permanently or temporarily as small children, schoolchildren or apprentices.

When Bona Taowere requested to foster her niece, this rule had not yet been well established. She thus had no idea that her request to foster the urban-born child of a civil servant from her village would be turned down. She took it for granted that her request would be fulfilled, otherwise she never would have asked. Thus she was shocked, ashamed and bitter for many, many years over the rejection, especially given that among the Baatombu a request which is turned down is considered very dishonourable for the one who made the request as well as for the one who declined. Grandparents no longer request to foster their urban grandchildren because they now fear, and in fact know, that they will be rejected. Due to the high rate of migration, people in the older generation inevitably have children or grandchildren living in urban areas. Often most of their descendents live there. The complaint that they can no longer foster their grandchildren refers to their experience with their urban relatives who no longer figure as a possible source of foster-children. This results in the often very real worry about social security for the older generation in the future. High population growth—in the three villages studied we found a completed fertility rate of 7.6 children—has so far guaranteed that enough people remain in the villages and can take care of the older generation in their homesteads. But I know of individual cases of people who work in the fields until a very old age because all their children live in the towns and none of their grandchildren is there to support them in the village. More men live without foster-sons than women without foster-daughters, which can be traced to the gender differences mentioned above and to the fact that women have a much greater interest in foster-children than men. Yet the general decline of child-fostering, which greatly affects fosterage on the part of grandparents, is one of the many transformations which are currently fundamentally changing the relationship between the generations in northern Benin.

REFERENCES

Alber, Erdmute. 2000. *Im Gewand von Herrschaft. Modalitäten der Macht bei den Baatombu (1895–1995)*. Köln: Rüdiger Köppe Verlag.

——2003. 'Denying biological parenthood: child fosterage in northern Benin', *Ethnos* 68 (4): 487–506.

Alber, Erdmute, and Jörn Sommer. 1999. 'Grenzen der Implementierung staatlichen Rechts im dörflichen Kontext. Eine Analyse der Rechtswirklichkeit in einem Baatombu-Dorf in Benin', *Afrika spectrum* 34 (1): 85–111.

Allman, Jean. 1997. 'Fathering, mothering and making sense of Ntamoba: reflections on the economy of child-rearing in colonial Asante', *Africa* 67 (2): 296–322.

Atto, Ursula. 1996. 'Verpflichtung, Belastung, Freude: Pflegekinder und ihr Verständnis der Hausarbeit', in Kurt Beck and Gerd Spittler (eds), *Arbeit in Afrika*. Hamburg: Lit Verlag.

Bledsoe, Caroline. 1980. 'The manipulation of Kpelle social fatherhood', *Ethnology* 19 (1): 29–47.

——1990. 'No success without struggle: social mobility and hardship for foster children in Sierra Leone', *Man* 25 (1): 70–88.

——2002. *Contingent Lives: fertility, time, and aging in West Africa*. Chicago and London: University of Chicago Press.

Bledsoe, Caroline and Anastasia Brandon. 1992. 'Child fosterage and child mortality in Sub-Saharan Africa: some preliminary questions and answers', in Étienne van de Walle, Gilles Pison, and Mpembele Sala-Diakanda (eds), *Mortality and Society in Sub-Saharan Africa*. Oxford: Clarendon Press.

Bledsoe, Caroline, and Uche Isingo-Abanike. 1989. 'Strategies of child-fosterage among Mende grannies in Sierra Leone', in Ron J. Lesthaeghe (ed.), *Reproduction and Social Organization in Sub-Saharan Africa*. Berkeley and London: University of California Press.

Carsten, Janet. 2000. 'Introduction: cultures of relatedness', in Janet Carsten (ed.), *Cultures of Relatedness: new approaches to the study of kinship*. Cambridge: Cambridge University Press.

Crowder, Michael. 1983. *Revolt in Bussa: a study of British native administration in Nigerian Borgu, 1902–1935*. London: Faber and Faber.

Fortes, Meyer. 1949. *The Web of Kinship among the Tallensi: the second part of an analysis of the social structure of a Trans-Volta Tribe*. London: Oxford University Press, for the International African Institute.

Goody, Esther N. 1982. *Parenthood and Social Reproduction: fostering and occupational roles in West Africa*. Cambridge: Cambridge University Press.

Goody, Jack. 1959. 'The mother's brother and the sister's son in West Africa', *Journal of the Royal Anthropological Institute* 59: 61–88.

Gottlieb, Alma. 1992. *Under the Kapok Tree: identity and difference in Beng thought*. Bloomington: Indiana University Press.

Isaac, Barry L., and R. Conrad Shelby. 1982. 'Child fosterage among the Mende of Upper Bambara Chiefdom, Sierra Leone: rural–urban and occupational comparisons', *Ethnology* 21 (3): 243–258.

Kuba, Richard. 1996. *Wasangari und Wangara. Borgu und seine Nachbarn in historischer Perspektive*. Hamburg: Lit Verlag.

Lallemand, Suzanne. 1993. *La circulation des enfants en société traditionelle. Prêt, don, échange*. Paris: L'Harmattan.

——1994. *Adoption et Mariage. Les Kotokoli du Centre du Togo*. Paris: L'Harmattan.

Lombard, Jacques. 1965. *Structures de type "feodal" en Afrique Noire. Etude des dynamismes internes et des relations sociales chez les Bariba du Dahomey.* Paris: Imprimerie Nationale.

Mannheim, Karl. 1928. 'Das Problem der Generationen', *Kölner Vierteljahrshefte für Soziologie* 7: 157–185.

Meier, Barbara. 1993. *Doglientiri. Frauengemeinschaften in westafrikanischen Verwandtschaftssystemen, dargestellt am Beispiel der Bulsa in Nordghana.* Münster: Lit Verlag.

——1999. 'Doglientiri: an institutionalised relationship between women among the Bulsa of northern Ghana', *Africa* 69 (1): 87–107.

Page, Hillary. 1989. 'Childrearing versus childbearing: coresidence of mother and child in Sub-Saharan Africa', in Ron J. Lesthaeghe (ed.), *Reproduction and Social Organization in Sub-Saharan Africa.* Berkeley and London: University of California Press.

Roost Vischer, Lilo. 1997. *Mütter zwischen Herd und Markt: das Verhältnis von Mutterschaft, sozialer Elternschaft und Frauenarbeit bei den Moose (Mossi) in Ouagadougou/Burkina Faso.* Basler Beiträge zur Ethnologie. Bd. 38. Basel: Ethnologisches Seminar der Universität und Museum der Kulturen.

Sargent, Carolyn F. 1982. *The Cultural Context of Therapeutic Choice: obstetrical care decisions among the Bariba of Benin.* Dordecht and London: Reidel.

——1988. 'Born to die: witchcraft and infanticide in Bariba Culture', *Ethnology* 27 (1): 79–95.

Schottman, Wendy. 1991. 'La Parole dans la vie sociale des Baatombu'. Doctoral thesis. Paris: Université Paris 5.

Shell-Duncan, Bettina K. 1994. 'Child fostering among nomadic Turkana pastoralists: demography and health consequences', in Elliot Fratkin, Kathleen Galvin and Eric Abella Roth (eds), *African Pastoralist Systems: an integrated approach.* Boulder CO: Lynne Rienner.

ABSTRACT

This article deals with an aspect of the special relationship between grandparents and grandchildren: the fosterage of grandchildren by their (classificatory) grandparents. By becoming social parents with full responsibility for their social children, grandparents—as foster-parents—take upon themselves the characteristics typical both of parental roles involving authority, and grand-parental behaviour involving joking, warmth and proximity to their fostered grandchildren. The practices of grandparental fosterage, as well as changes in them, need to be understood in the broader context of widespread fosterage among Baatombu, where the majority of children grow up not with their bio-logical parents but with foster-parents. The gradual decline of old forms of fosterage is affecting foster practices between grandparents and grandchildren. The grandparents' generation evaluate this decline negatively and fear that changing fosterage patterns may adversely affect their social security in old age.

RÉSUMÉ

Cet article traite d'un aspect de la relation particulière entre grands-parents et petits-enfants : la prise en charge des petits-enfants par leurs grands-parents (classificatoires). En devenant des parents sociaux pleinement responsables de leurs enfants sociaux, les grands-parents, en tant que parents nourriciers, adoptent les caractéristiques typiques à la fois des rôles parentaux faisant intervenir l'autorité et du comportement grand-parental faisant intervenir la plaisanterie, la chaleur et la proximité avec les petits-enfants dont ils ont la charge. Les pratiques de prise en charge grand-parentale, ainsi que leur évolution, sont à appréhender dans le contexte plus large de la pratique répandue du placement d'enfants chez les Baatombu, où la majorité des enfants grandissent non pas avec leurs parents biologiques, mais avec des parents nourriciers. Le recul progressif des anciennes formes de placement affecte actuellement les pratiques d'accueil entre grands-parents et petits-enfants. La génération des grands-parents voit ce recul de façon négative et craint que l'évolution des modèles d'accueil n'ait un effet négatif sur sa sécurité sociale lorsqu'elle sera vieille.

GRANDPARENTS AND GRANDCHILDREN IN KWAHU, GHANA: THE PERFORMANCE OF RESPECT

Sjaak van der Geest

'Unlucky the house that does not have an old person living in it.'

INTRODUCTION

This description of relations between grandparents and grandchildren in a Ghanaian community argues that the quality of these relations varies according to age and gender. Literature on African kinship has almost entirely focused on very young grandchildren. This article draws attention to changes that occur when those children grow into adolescents and adults. The second argument is about performance: kinship and relatedness need to be demonstrated in public even when their 'content' has dwindled.

Several young people quoted the proverb used as an epigraph for this article, when I asked them about their views on older people. Their answer confirmed an established truth that an old person is wise and can guide the relatives in the house. I raised the question during research on social and cultural aspects of growing old in Kwahu-Tafo, a rural town in southern Ghana.

Fieldwork

The fieldwork mainly consisted of conversations with about thirty-five older people and their relatives or household members. Some of these conversations were lengthy, others short and casual. I met frequently with some older people, with others only a few times. All conversations, except the very casual ones, were taped, transcribed and translated into English. Only a few were conducted in English. Additional insights were acquired through participant observation, short visits and discussions with young people about the old. Finally, I conducted some research in various schools in Kwahu-Tafo and its surrounding towns involving questionnaires, incomplete sentence tests and drawings of an older person.

The town of Kwahu-Tafo

Kwahu-Tafo is situated in the Eastern Region and has over 5,000 inhabitants. It is a town like many others in the area, though slightly

SJAAK VAN DER GEEST is Professor of Medical Anthropology at the University of Amsterdam. He has done fieldwork in Ghana and Cameroon on a variety of subjects including the use and distribution of medicines. His other interests include highlife song texts, the meanings of growing old, and concepts of dirt and defecation.

more impoverished and dilapidated. Its inhabitants as in all Kwahu towns are mobile. They love trading, that is, buying things in one place and retailing them in another, and can be found over the whole country. For people of the older generation, men as well as women, the 'normal' life cycle consisted of growing up in Kwahu-Tafo, then travelling and trading in one of the commercial centres of the country and finally returning to their hometown to settle as a farmer (cf. Bartle 1977). That life cycle is less common nowadays as most people of the younger generation aspire to careers other than trading and farming, but the mobility still prevails.

Old and young in Kwahu-Tafo

For young people in Kwahu-Tafo having an old person in the house almost necessarily implies living with a grandparent. A survey among school pupils aged between twelve and eighteen showed that more than two-thirds of them had in fact an older person living in the same house. The percentage may seem high but was lower than I had expected, taking into account that three—if not four—generations constitute the 'natural' composition of a household. There is indeed something unnatural about a house accommodating only two generations.

Children are most likely to live in the same house as their maternal grandmother. Kwahu people, who belong to the matrilineal Akan, prefer to stay on in their maternal home after their marriage, if that is possible. Clearly, that is difficult if the marital partners are from different towns, but it *is* possible when they are both from Kwahu-Tafo. In that case the woman is most likely to continue staying with her mother and conduct her marital duties from there. It mainly boils down to cooking food for her husband in her mother's house and bringing it—or sending a child to bring it—to her husband in *his* family house. In the night she may go to her husband's room to sleep with him. When a man is able to build his own house or rent a decent apartment, his wife will probably join him, but she dislikes the idea of living with her in-laws. Conversely, for a man it is even more difficult to stay with his wife's relatives in one house. Others will laugh at him and consider him a failure.

The concept of grandparent (*Nana*) is classificatory and children make little or no distinction between their biological and other 'grandparents'. They may even not be aware of the fact that the *Nana* in the house is not their 'real' grandmother but their grandmother's sister or cousin or a more distant relative. For the purpose of this essay I assume that the interactions between first and third generations that I observed and discussed in the households I visited were in fact grandparent–grandchild interactions in the broad sense of the word.

NANA KWAKU AGYEI

Nana Kwaku Agyei was one of the first older people I contacted when I started my fieldwork on old age in 1994. I was walking with a friend when we met him. We greeted him respectfully and he replied with a request: could we give him some money to buy food? We told him we would come and visit him later in the day to have a conversation. He promised to wait for us and so he did. It was the beginning of a friendship that lasted only one year, till his death in 1995.

Kwaku Agyei was not a successful and highly respected elder. He was poor, to start with. He did not even have a proper place to stay and had begged some people if he could live in an empty room in their house until his nephew had finished the house he was building for him and his sisters. It was a small room in an old and rickety mud house with some of its walls collapsed. Agyei's room contained only a bed and a chair. Some clothes were hanging on big nails in the walls. The blankets on the bed were threadbare and dirty. These blankets, his trousers and long-sleeved shirt were gifts from the Polish Catholic parish priest.

After his death people blamed him for his poverty. They said he had lived carelessly and never become a proper farmer. He had been lazy and had done little for his children. During his active years he had been the town's gong-gong beater, a messenger of the chief whose task was to make announcements, for example on communal labour or special events. For the rest he had been hanging around in the chief's palace hoping to get some money from people visiting the chief for judicial matters. His wife had left him after thirty-two years of marriage because, as she explained to me, he always quarrelled with her. According to him the real reason was that he was poor and unable to support her.

Kwaku Agyei was a witty person, in spite of his misery. His experiences in the chief's court had filled him with wisdom and an impressive knowledge of traditional customs. He was particularly fond of proverbs and when he found out that I enjoyed listening to them he cleverly exploited that knowledge to impress me and my friends. When I asked him for the meaning of a proverb that I had heard or read about, he never was at a loss. I noticed that he readily produced explanations even for proverbs that he had never heard before. One of his (and my) favourite ones was: 'If the old person has nothing, he has elbow' (*Ɔpanyin nni biribi a, ɔwɔ abatwɛ*), meaning even if the old person has nothing, he has wisdom. The proverb suited his condition and became some kind of personal motto.[1]

Every night a young girl of about five came to the old man's room and kept him company during the night. She was his granddaughter, his favourite daughter's child, who lived about 500 metres away. The girl also did small errands for her grandfather and emptied his chamber pot in the morning. Agyei affectionately called her *me yere* ('my wife').

My reason for introducing Kwaku Agyei at this stage is that his life in old age and his position as elder and grandparent epitomise several features of grandparents and their relationship with grandchildren that will be discussed further on. His accommodation was unusual but in many other respects he was 'typical' in keeping up the appearance of

---

[1] For a discussion on the various interpretations of this proverb, see Van der Geest (1996).

being an elder who is respected by his grandchildren and admired for his wisdom and knowledge of tradition.

The little girl, 'his wife', was sent by her mother and was not particularly close to the old man. She was just respectful and obedient. I observed Agyei's behaviour towards other grandchildren and found him often peevish and mean to them. One incident I remember particularly well. A small girl was attending him while he was eating. He gave her brusque instructions. The girl politely did everything he told her. When he finished eating he gave her the tiny last bit of the soup. She drank it and then brought him water to drink and wash his hands.

When she put the small piece of soap on the balustrade, he grumbled that she should put it elsewhere. She moved it 30 cm. She dried the floor with a rag and swept it. Kwaku Agyei and his two sisters simultaneously shouted at her: *To wo boase* ('Do calmly'). Apparently she caused too much dust. It suddenly occurred to me that Kwaku Agyei was not the cheerful, gentle and humorous old man he always was to me. I found him rather unkind to others, particularly to children.

I visited Kwaku Agyei about thirty times in the last year of his life, sometimes for a long conversation, which we recorded (and transcribed later on), sometimes just to say hello and have a chat. I never saw any grandchild engaged in a conversation with him. The only person who was interested in his wisdom was I, the anthropologist. I recall one day that we were discussing certain proverbs about old age when a young woman staying in the house came closer to listen to our conversation. We asked her if she had learned any proverbs from the old man and she answered in the negative. Agyei confirmed her answer and added: 'She will not learn proverbs because the proverbs will not earn her any money.' It was an indirect conclusion that young people were no longer interested in the wisdom of their grandparents, because it did not contain anything 'useful' for them.

Kwaku Agyei is the main character in an essay I wrote about the concept of *ɔpanyin* ('elder') in Kwahu society (Van der Geest 1998). There I argued that his love for proverbs which extolled the virtues of the old person was a way of keeping up his faith in the beauty of old age, while knowing that it had already lost most of its charm, certainly in the eyes of the third generation.

TERMS AND CLICHÉS

Nana (plural: *nananom*) is the term for grandparent, whether grandmother or grandfather, whether maternal or paternal. The term, as I have already indicated, is used for any other relative of the same generation as the grandparents. The term is reciprocal: grandparents call their grandchildren *nana* as well (but pronounced slightly differently). Ancestors are also addressed by the term *nana*, for example when pouring libation.[2] Finally, *nana* is an honorific term, a title of respect one

---

[2] For a description of the Akan libation ritual, see Adjaye (2001).

could use for any older or important person, particularly for the chief and the members of his council.

When one asks anyone how grandparents and grandchildren relate to each other, one is likely to get the answer that their relationship is extremely warm and positive. In the classic functionalist collection *African Systems of Kinship and Marriage* (Radcliffe-Browne and Forde 1950), Fortes wrote a contribution about kinship and marriage in Asante society, which is very close—geographically and culturally—to Kwahu. His remarks of half a century ago could still count as today's stereotype:

> The grandparents ... on both sides are the most honoured of all one's kinfolk. Their position and status are of very great importance in the social system... The maternal grandmother ... is the guardian of morals and of harmony in the household... It is from the grandparents of both sexes that children learn family history, folklore, proverbs and other traditional lore... The grandparents ... are looked up to with reverence, not only as the repositories of ancient wisdom but also as symbols of the continuity of descent. [Fortes 1950: 276]

My friend and co-researcher Obeng Boamah also stressed the close relationship between grandchildren and grandparents:

> Some children like staying with their grandparents because they are more sympathetic, patient and caring. They may give them more food than they would enjoy from the cooking pot of their mother. They are freer when they stay with their grandparents.

There are also disadvantages, however, as Boamah remarked: 'The children may be less well trained [as they will be spoiled]. They may not perform household duties as well [as children staying with their parents].' And finally the old stereotype: 'Children learn culture and tradition from their grandparents. Grandparents show them the boundary of the farm.[3] Some may give their grandchildren money of gold dust and tell them stories and proverbs.'

My fieldwork in Kwahu-Tafo enabled me to look critically at the rosy accounts of the close relationship between grandparents and grandchildren. I will do so by examining both the attitudes and actions of the grandparents and those of the grandchildren, but first we shall sketch how older people see themselves vis-à-vis the young and how members of the young generation look upon their grandparents.

HOW DO GRANDPARENTS SEE THEMSELVES?

My conversations with older people were of two kinds. One kind focused on the pains and worries of growing old: poor health, poverty,

---

[3] This remark is derived from a proverb that indicates that only the old people know the boundaries of the farm. So, if one does not accompany the old people to the farm, one may later on be cheated by neighbours who will take some of the family land away.

loneliness, boredom, lack of care, lack of respect, loss of friends. The other type emphasised the pleasure and beauty of old age: being old was in itself a positive achievement; it entailed an accumulation of life experience and good manners which engendered respect and affection in children and grandchildren. The first type can largely be interpreted as an indirect critique of others who made them suffer, the second as self-praise. For a self-portrait of older people we should therefore focus on the second type of conversations.

There are four terms in Twi which are commonly used for people of old age. In the case of a man these terms are: *ɔpanyin*, *akokora*, *akokora pɔsɔpɔsɔ* and *nana*. For a woman these are: *ɔbaa pinyin*, *aberewa*, *aberewa pɔsɔpɔsɔ* and *nana*. The old people themselves prefer the first term. An *ɔpanyin*—or for that matter *ɔbaa panyin*—is an older person who is still vital in mind and, to a certain extent, body. The term can best be translated as 'elder', which implies seniority and has the connotation of wisdom and social importance. *Akokora* or *aberewa* is more associated with bodily—and mental—weakness as a result of advanced age and this association is even more explicit if the adjective *pɔsɔpɔsɔ* ('shaky', 'infirm') is added. *Nana*, as we have seen, is again a very positive word, mostly used as a term of address, expressing respect. When I asked an old man what shows that someone is *ɔpanyin*, he replied:

> You can see it in the wisdom he passes on to the young and in the way he respects himself. If you respect yourself, the young will also respect you and give you everything you need... An *ɔpanyin* does not drink, behaves well and shows respect to the young.

The proverbs that we discussed in our conversations implied many positive qualities of older people. The most important one was their wisdom and life experience, which enabled them to predict the future and advise younger people. The fact that one has lived for a long time implies that one has seen a lot of things and understands how they are related, why one event follows another. This wisdom enables the old person to foresee misfortune and tell people how they can prevent it from happening. When I asked one of the older people what marked the difference between them and young people, he answered: 'Wisdom, the capacity to think before acting. Young people just begin to act without thinking.' That wisdom and capacity to look ahead endows the old person also with power. That is why a proverb says *Ɔpanyin ano sen ɔbosom* ('The mouth of an elder is stronger than god').

The *ɔpanyin* also has good manners that are rooted in self-restraint. He is in control of his emotions, he does not become angry and does not shout at people. His self-discipline also shows in his attitude to food, drink, sex and other physical pleasures. Gluttony and greediness do no befit an older person. One elder said: 'If there is not enough food in the house, the *ɔpanyin* gives his portion to the children.' Another added:

> We have a proverb, *Ɔpanyin yam adwansae aduasa* ['There are thirty sheep in the stomach of the *ɔpanyin*']. You know it is your food but that child has nothing to eat. You tell him he can eat it. I can chew kola and get satisfied.

The ɔpanyin has lived his life, he has eaten so much in this world. All he needs to do now is to look after his people in the house.

Wisdom, caution, discipline and altruism are the main virtues of the older people (in their own eyes). These virtues are kept together by their dedication to the family (*abusua*). The ɔpanyin is concerned about only one thing: the well-being of the *abusua*. His life is drawing to an end and soon he will join the ancestors. There is no reason to worry about material things. Only his children and grandchildren count. One old man explained:

> An ɔpanyin should not travel or go and live somewhere else. He should stay at home and offer advice to the young. If there is a conflict in the house, he will reconcile the two parties. If an ɔpanyin goes to travel and live somewhere else, people will criticise him and call him a bad ɔpanyin [ɔpanyin bofoɔ]. It is the duty of an ɔpanyin to stay at home, advise relatives and re-establish peace.

The well-being of the *abusua* is the touchstone of everything the ɔpanyin undertakes. Whatever he does, if it benefits the family, it is good. If it does not, he will be criticised. His wisdom is meant for the *abusua*. His refusal to entertain gossip holds the family together. His unselfishness and patience are an example for others in the house.

Of course, the older people know this is an idealistic picture, but they believe in the ideal. They *have* lived long and dispose of a considerable amount of experience, so they are entitled to the respect and attention of their children and grandchildren.

HOW DO YOUNG PEOPLE VIEW THEIR GRANDPARENTS?

Interestingly, young people confirmed the positive view of the older people about their own qualities. One of the most remarkable 'proofs' of that positive view I experienced during a few discussions with young men aged around eighteen. I asked them what they meant when they said—as they had been doing—that they respected older people. One of them answered:

> The meaning of the respect we have for the old is that the old are far more advanced in years than we. So, when you get nearer to them and respect them, they will reveal to you how they got to that age and they will tell you traditions and customs that will enable you also to reach that age.

Another young informant remarked:

> The meaning of respect is getting nearer to the old and giving them the necessary honour. Moreover, we think that the aged have a certain blessing because of their mere age, and so when you respect and honour them and

they bless you, it will be forever on your life. In much the same way, when they curse you, it will also be forever.

I asked them how they showed their respect and invited them to give concrete examples of respectful behaviour in their own house. One of them said:

It is something that we the Akan have done over the years and which has come to stay. White men have a different lifestyle. I have some relatives who were born and bred in Canada and came back home recently. When they are engaged in a work and you call them, they will not mind you because they want to use their time according to their personal plans without interruption. But Akan are not like this. Even when you are asleep and an old person calls you, you cannot ignore him. Whether you like it or not, you have to wake up and attend to his call. Respect is our tradition. If you are not obeying that tradition, they will call you a bad child. Every child should show respect, especially to the old people in the house. In my own house, I have two old persons. One of them called us today, and asked us whether we know we are his grandchildren and so every morning, when we wake up from bed, the first thing we have to do is to come to his room, greet him, ask his condition of life. In case something is worrying him, we will be the first to know this. If we didn't do all these things, it would not be good.

Another performance of respect was presented during a 'test' of uncompleted sentences which school pupils (mainly male) in Kwahu-Tafo and two nearby places filled in for me. One sentence started with: 'My grandfather... ' Out of eighty-three entries (some multiple), only two made a (partly) negative remark, six referred to the old man's physical weakness, five mentioned his need of help, the same number made a remark about being in need of help approaching death, and one said he resembled a child. All other entries were either neutral (for example, simply revealing his name) or positive: giving advice (6), telling stories (6), helping others in the house (8), still working hard (10) and references to respect and kindness. A few examples (slightly corrected for English language) illustrate their views:

My grandfather is very good because he taught me how to be a good child in any way. [Male, 17 years, no. 9]

My grandfather is a person who knows things about the past. So anytime my grandfather visits us, it is a great day for me because he tells me stories about the past and advises me on certain behaviours. [Male, 16 years, no. 91]

My grandfather is a very old person in my house and head of the family. He is very popular in the community for the good work he has done for the people living in the community. [Male, 19 years, no. 140]

One respondent was more ambivalent:

My grandfather was ... [unclear] ... a hardworking farmer. During his lifetime he worked hard to reach the demands of the whole family and loved everybody. The only thing, which I disliked about him was that he smoked and drank alcoholic drinks which was against the Bible. He also appreciated material things. [Male, 17 years, no. 60]

The role of adviser and helper was still more strongly expressed in sentences starting with 'My grandmother ... '. Out of 79 entries, 13 mentioned her good advice, 10 her story-telling, 11 her kindness, 6 her help to others in the house and 4 the fact that she was still working very hard. A few examples (English slightly corrected):

My grandmother is good for me because she told me about the past and taught me important things. [Female, 17 years, no. 236]

My grandmother told me not to make friends who will lead me into disaster. But I paid no need to what she said and my life ended in disaster. [Male, 20 years, no. 172]

My grandmother loves her grandchildren, especially me. She likes telling me stories and sometimes gives me money for food. She likes calling my name because I am her youngest grandchild. [Male, 18 years, no. 116]

My grandmother is the best woman I have ever seen. She is kind and generous. She cares very much for me, especially during my mother's absence. She also advises me and used to tell me old tales. I always love her. [Male, 17 years, no. 85]

The contrast between these professions of affection and communication between young people and their grandparents and my daily observations was remarkable. These young people in their late teens assured me that they benefited from the presence of older persons in the house. They said they enjoyed their stories about the past and their knowledge of traditional lore and listened to their advice on important issues in life. When I asked them about specific meetings and conversations with grandparents, I soon found out that they did not occur. During my frequent visits to older people I had the same experience: I never saw a young person of the age of my informants involved in a conversation with an older person in the house. The older people confirmed this: their grandchildren did not come to them for any kind of advice. It was only small children below the age of ten who could be seen in the company of their grandparents talking to them.

The accounts of the adolescents should not be disregarded as false information, however. They should be taken seriously, not as reliable reports about what actually happens, but as demonstrations of the respect that youngsters owe their grandparents. If they uttered phrases of ideal behaviour—or referred to their behaviour of ten years ago—it was because that was the way they should speak about older people. It was a way of showing respect, courteousness, and politeness. The contrast between publicly expressed respect and privately held indifference or even resentment, led me to examine the mechanics of respect and reciprocity in the context of the family.

THE MECHANICS OF RESPECT AND RECIPROCITY

In her introduction to a recent collection of essays on kinship Janet Carsten (2000) suggests the concept of relatedness. Taking her inspiration from the work of David Schneider she wants to rekindle the interest in kinship among anthropologists by linking it to discussions on the cultural meaning of 'nature' or 'biology'. Biology, blood relationship, provides the primary mode of expressing connection. Apart from its symbolic efficacy, 'blood' stands for 'first contact', the first sharing of food and body fluids. Kinship is the first social ordering in which people find themselves and is therefore an important determinant of a sense of 'belonging'. But the ordering itself is not enough; it is a space which needs to be filled by tangible signs of relatedness: giving and receiving, mutual dependence, reciprocal exchanges concerning material, cognitive and emotional matters. If practical reciprocity does not enter the domain of kinship, relatedness remains void and shrivels. Kinship needs to be practiced in solidarity, mutual assistance. If this does not happen, relatedness will seek its way outside the circle of blood relations.

To have something in common forms the basis of relatedness. Sharing and exchanging goods, services, emotions, reproduction and meaning, constitute the 'stuff' out of which kinship relations are made. The family stands as a model of fertile reciprocity. It is often used, therefore, as a metaphor for other groups in which people practice reciprocity in a gratifying manner: associations, religious groups, and even the state.

Carsten quotes Marilyn Strathern who calls kinship 'the social recognition of the actual facts of biological relatedness' (Strathern 1995: 222, quoted in Carsten 2000: 9). I accept that way of putting it, but want to emphasise that biological relatedness only becomes relatedness in the true sense of the word if it develops social and cultural values for sharing. That is why I prefer to see blood relationship as the first and most directly available opportunity for exchange of the things that people need in life. We may call it the first invitation to reciprocity. Kinship is the naturalisation of relatedness. But if the reciprocity leaks away, kinship becomes an atrophy or at best a memory.

It is time I expounded the concept of reciprocity. It is one of those concepts that are so fundamental to social and cultural life that they refract from attempts to define them. Gouldner (1996: 47 f.) presents a list of renowned social scientists (Simmel, Hobhouse, and Becker, to mention a few) who viewed reciprocity as the basis of all forms of social organisation, but failed to define it. The most enlightening and comprehensive discussion of reciprocity is probably *The Gift: an interdisciplinary perspective* (Komter 1996). The contributions are from anthropologists, sociologists, social psychologists and economists.

All authors in Aafke Komter's interdisciplinary collection of readings on reciprocity emphasise that human relations and interactions derive form and substance from the game of giving and receiving. Early anthropologists stressed that this exchange of objects and services brought about a moral community. Others, Bourdieu for example, pointed out the symbolic meaning of reciprocity: people express who they are in the presents and care they give to each other. Some hold the view that reciprocity entails a careful calculation and should be understood as self-interest, either short or long term. Others stress its unselfish character: people give without calculation; they sacrifice themselves without asking a reward.

Following these different accents Komter distinguishes four types of human actors: *homo moralis, homo symbolicus, homo economicus,* and *homo generosus.* These distinctions suggest too much difference, however. There is a subtle economy in generosity. The mother who takes care of her sick child, acts spontaneously, without any calculation, but she does get a reward: the child's gratitude. Moreover, she has created a moral fact that will move the child to look after its mother when she needs it. Obviously, symbolic expressions of belonging, affection and family identity work alongside this exchange of care. These different and complementary perspectives show that reciprocity can assume various forms and meanings but remain the basis *and* content of human relations. Every communication and interaction should be understood as a form of reciprocity. The statement is close to tautological; without reciprocity it would not be communication or interaction.

How does this relate to the theme of this paper? My point is that the reciprocity between grandparents and grandchildren in Kwahu-Tafo is slowly 'drying up' and that this process is not well understood by anthropologists. That the crumbling of reciprocity between grandparents and grandchildren has been overlooked in studies of old age in Africa is mainly due to the fact that students only had eyes for very young grandchildren. The relatively few studies of grandparent–grandchild relationships have indeed focused on situations where the degree of reciprocity is very high, that is when grandchildren are small and in need of the things that grandparents have in abundance: attention, love, tenderness. Conversely young grandchildren provide their grandparents with opportunities to redo their past lives and enjoy the pleasures of children for whom they may not have had the time and maturity when they were young parents.

If, however, we focus our attention on the relationship between grown-up grandchildren and their—still older—grandparents, we are likely to view a very different situation. The blood relationship is there, but its reciprocal contents, emotions, life experience, communication, may have leaked away. The wisdom of the grandparents may no longer have relevance to the young generation. Their knowledge regarding farming, medicinal herbs, traditional customs, stories of the past and ancestors has grown obsolete in the eyes of the young. The new generation needs other types of knowledge to survive and become successful in life: school education, knowledge of how to contact the right person to acquire a job or a visa to go abroad. Grandparents have little in common with their grown-up grandchildren and exchange of information decreases. Reciprocity becomes redundant and dwindles to the performance of respect.

Am I too rigid in my reading of reciprocity? Is the relative uninterest of teenagers and older adolescents in their grandparents not a 'normal' phenomenon and, moreover, very widespread? Is it not a temporary phase which will pass when the grandchildren get children themselves and have topics and things (children) to share with their grandparents? And do they, during that period of low tide, not have memories of their childhood in which grandparents played a central role? Should we conclude that there is 'nothing' between grandchildren and grandparents if we do not *observe* communication and shared activities between them?

Elders complained to me that their grandchildren did not come to them. Do I perhaps take that complaint too seriously? Have older people not always been saying that the young do not listen to them? Cattell (1994, 1997) describes the growing gap between grandmothers and granddaughters in Kenya, and Møller and Sotshongaye (2002) write about the loss of respect felt by grandmothers in South Africa. Both articles place their observations in the framework of 'complaint discourse'. That is what older people normally do: complain (see Sagner 2002). Elsewhere in this issue, Benedicte Ingstad's quote from Schapera (1940: 265 f.) shows the same complaint about lack of respect in the 1930s. Young people, for their part, have always been saying that life has changed and that the old do not understand the new facts of life. So, why not treat their words as styles of generational parlance instead of factual information?

These are hard questions I put to myself. Answering them will necessarily contain some speculation. I do indeed think that men in particular are witnessing changes that are far more profound than those reported in the 1930s, 1950s and 1970s. Fewer young men than ever before follow in the footsteps of their fathers, let alone their grandfathers. Practical reciprocity that implies discussing relevant matters of life will continue to decline in their case. In the case of granddaughters, however, there may be more overlap in interests with their mothers and grandmothers. When they move into motherhood and have children of their own, this will bring new 'stuff' to fill the relation with their grandmothers. Moreover, grandmothers usually played a greater role in the childhood years of their grandchildren than grandfathers. Reviving memories and reactivating long-term reciprocity will focus first of all on grandmothers.

Politeness and good manners is what is left over of the warm and busy reciprocity that characterised the relationship between small grandchildren and their grandfathers. This type of respect serves its purpose: it enables the older men to keep faith in their own excellence and protects the young against public criticism and the dangers of cursing and witchcraft which the old may use to hurt them. Indeed, a large part of my fieldwork data were demonstrations of respect which were designed to keep up the ideal picture of the wise and celebrated grandparents who, in Fortes' words, 'are looked up to with reverence ... as the repositories of ancient wisdom' (1950: 276).

Respect, one could say, is a compromise, a strategy to deal with the disappearance of practical reciprocity. It is a strategy because it allows both generations to retain their dignity and—to some extent—their relatedness. Behind that appearance of mutual respect, however, resentment and loneliness may lie, as I have described elsewhere (Van der Geest 2002, 2004). I am not suggesting that reciprocal activities are 'real' while respect is some kind of fake façade. I do not see a split between ideology and actual practice. Performing respect in speaking is as much an activity as practising it in sharing a meal, giving money or asking advice. The point, however, is that the older people make distinctions between the 'doing' of respect and other forms of communication and reciprocity. It is the absence of communication (advice, family history, traditional wisdom) that worries them.

One of the elders in Kwahu-Tafo remarked that there was no greater happiness for him than a young person who would come to him and ask a question. The implication is clear: the fact that young people do not come to listen to their stories and advice constitutes their main doubt about the quality of their relatedness.

ACKNOWLEDGEMENTS

The research for this paper was carried out with the help of many people. Most prominent was the assistance given by my Ghanaian co-researchers Kwame Fosu, Samuel Sarkodie, Patrick Atuobi and Anthony Obeng Boamah. Benjamin Boadi and Yaw Darko Ansah typed most of the research material. I am also indebted to Kofi Ron Lange, Sera Young, Geertje van der Geest, Erdmute Alber, Wenzel Geissler and Susan Reynolds Whyte for various kinds of support. Last, but not least, I would like to thank the old people who shared their knowledge and concerns with me and the young who expressed to me their respect for their grandparents.

REFERENCES

Adjaye, J. K. 2001. 'The performativity of Akan libations: an ethnopoetic construction of reality', *Ghana Studies* 4: 107–138.

Apt, N. A. 1996. *Coping with Old Age in a Changing Africa: social change and the elderly Ghanaian*. Aldershot: Avebury.

Bartle, P. 1977. 'Urban Migration and Rural Identity: an ethnography of a Kwawu community'. Ph.D. thesis. Legon: University of Ghana.

Carsten, J. 2000. 'Introduction: cultures of relatedness', in J. Carsten (ed.), *Cultures of Relatedness: new approaches to the study of kinship*. Cambridge: Cambridge University Press.

Cattell, M. G. 1994. ' "Nowadays it isn't easy to advise the young": grandmothers and granddaughters among Abaluyia of Kenya', *Journal of Cross-Cultural Gerontology* 9 (2): 157–78.

——1997. 'The discourse of neglect: family support for the elderly in Samia', in T. S. Weisner, C. Bradley, and P. L. Kilbride (eds), *African Families and the Crisis of Social Change*. Westport CT and London: Bergin & Garvey.

Fortes, M. 1950. 'Kinship and marriage among the Ashanti', in A. R. Radcliffe-Browne and D. Forde (eds), *African Systems of Kinship and Marriage*. London: Oxford University Press, for the International African Institute.

Gouldner, A. W. 1996. 'The norm of reciprocity: a preliminary statement', in A. E. Komter (ed.), *The Gift: an interdisciplinary perspective*. Amsterdam: Amsterdam University Press.

Komter, A. E. 1996. 'Introduction', in A. E. Komter (ed.), *The Gift: an interdisciplinary perspective*. Amsterdam: Amsterdam University Press.

Møller, V., and A. Sotshongaye. 2002. ' "They don't listen": contemporary respect relations between Zulu grandmothers and grandchildren', in S. Makoni and K. Stroeken (eds), *Ageing in Africa: sociolinguistic and anthropological approaches*. Aldershot: Ashgate.

Radcliffe-Browne, A. R., and D. Forde (eds). 1950. *African Systems of Kinship and Marriage*. London: Oxford University Press, for the International African Institute.

Sagner, A. 2002. 'Identity management and old age construction among Xhosa-speakers in urban South Africa: complaint discourse revisited', in S. Makoni and K. Stroeken (eds), *Ageing in Africa: sociolinguistic and anthropological approaches*. Aldershot: Ashgate.

Schapera, I. 1940. *Married Life in an African Tribe*. London: Faber and Faber.

Strathern, M. 1995. *The Relation: issues in complexity and scale*. Prickly Pear Pamphlet no. 6. Cambridge: Prickly Pear Press.

Van der Geest, S. 1996. 'The elder and his elbow: twelve interpretations of an Akan proverb', *Research in African Literatures* 27 (3): 110–18.

——1998. 'Ɔpanyin: the ideal of elder in the Akan culture of Ghana', *Canadian Journal of African Studies* 32 (3): 449–93.

——2002. 'From wisdom to witchcraft: ambivalence towards old age in rural Ghana', *Africa* 72 (3): 437–63.

——2004. ' "They don't come to listen": the experience of loneliness among older people in Kwahu, Ghana', *Journal of Cross-Cultural Gerontology* 19 (2).

ABSTRACT

This description of relations between grandparents and grandchildren in a rural Ghanaian community argues that the quality of these relations varies according to age and gender. Literature on African kinship has almost entirely focused on very young grandchildren. This article draws attention to changes that occur when those children grow into adolescents and adults. Grandchildren—both young and old—speak respectfully about their grandparents, but older people regret that their grandchildren do not come to them for advice once they have grown up. Older men seem more 'neglected' by their grandchildren than older women. The second argument is about performance: respect, affection and relatedness between grandparents and grandchildren are demonstrated in public even when their 'contents' have dwindled. The article is based on anthropological fieldwork over a period of almost ten years.

RÉSUMÉ

Cette description des relations entre grands-parents et petits-enfants dans une communauté rurale ghanéenne montre que la qualité de ces relations varie selon l'âge et le sexe. La littérature consacrée à la parenté africaine s'est presque exclusivement intéressée aux petits-enfants en bas âge. Cet article attire l'attention sur les changements qui surviennent lorsque ces enfants deviennent adolescents et adultes. Les petits-enfants, jeunes et vieux, parlent respectueusement de leurs grands-parents, mais les personnes âgées regrettent que leurs petits-enfants, une fois adultes, ne viennent plus leur demander conseil. Les hommes âgés semblent plus «négligés» par leurs petits-enfants que les femmes âgées. Le second argument concerne la conduite : respect, affection et parenté entre grands-parents et petits-enfants se manifestent en public même lorsque leur «contenu» s'est réduit. L'article repose sur des études anthropologiques de terrain qui se sont déroulées sur une période de près de dix ans.

THE VALUE OF GRANDCHILDREN: CHANGING RELATIONS BETWEEN GENERATIONS IN BOTSWANA

Benedicte Ingstad

The relationship between the generations, and in particular that between grandparents and grandchildren, has been changing in Botswana as a result of developments since Independence in 1966. In this article I will argue that in order to understand these changes one cannot look at grandparents–grandchildren as one unified type of relationship. We must distinguish between grandmothers and grandfathers and their relationships to various categories of grandchildren.

Following this argument I will discuss these relationships according to Charles Taylor's definition of *moral space* (1989) and see how the grandchildren may (or may not) contribute to the axes of *respect, meaning* and *dignity* for their grandparents. According to Taylor, personal and social identities are developed and sustained in a relationship to others, and through a common understanding, which is embedded in practices of the society (Taylor 1985a, 1985b). Thus the way people are seen and treated by others will also affect the way they see themselves. A culturally rooted perception of the older person as someone to be respected and cared for can only be sustained in the long run if younger people actually are willing to behave in ways that confirm this picture. *Moral space* is not only concerned with rights and duties as such, but with what is considered the right behaviour. Taylor claims that the three moral axes may be found in all societies, with a varying relationship to each other and with varying emphases. *Respect* has mainly to do with rights and duties: what we are expected to give to others, but also what we expect to receive from people around us. *Meaning* has to do with what makes life worth living. *Dignity* consists of the honour we expect as persons, our power to dominate public space or our self sufficiency (Taylor 1985a: 15). These are not independent dimensions. What happens along one influences the others. According to Taylor these axes are to be found in all societies. What varies from culture to culture is the content given to them and how they are evaluated in relation to each other. According to to Taylor, modern society is characterised by placing more emphasis on respect (for instance individual human rights) and less on dignity. By studying moral space, and how the emphasis on these values vary, Taylor claims that we can do an historical analysis of developments in

BENEDICTE INGSTAD is a Professor of Medical Anthropology at the Department of General Practice and Community Medicine, University of Oslo, Norway. She has carried out anthropological fieldwork in Greenland, Norway and Botswana (among the Tswana and the San people). Her main fields of interest are disability in a cross-cultural perspective, care for the elderly, traditional medicine and traditional healing, and migration and health.

one single society, as well as a cross-cultural comparison of different societies (Fossland and Grimen 2001).

The aim of this article is to study the development of moral space over time, in relation to a particular topic (the relationship between grandparents and grandchildren) and in one specific country (Botswana). There have been structural and social changes over the years that clearly have an impact on the relationship between the young and the old. However, the emphasis in this article will be more on changes as experienced by the elderly people themselves in their *moral space* than on what may be considered 'historical facts'. Elderly people everywhere seem to have a tendency to idealise the past when it comes to describing the relationship between the young and the old. While this picture may be lacking in historical accuracy it has important bearings on their perception of their present life situation.

BACKGROUND

Botswana today is in many ways a modern society but also one with many contrasts: between the poor and the rich, the urban and the rural as well as between hope and despair. At the time of Independence (1966) ranked among the poorest countries in the world, Botswana has in many ways become a success story among the developing nations. It has seen an average 9% economic growth annually, one of the highest in the world, and is now considered a middle-income country. It has close to universal primary school attendance and a well-developed junior secondary school system, which aims to give every child the option of a minimum of ten years education. It also has a well-developed primary health care system with the intention to serve all citizens within walking distance of their homes. These remarkable developments have taken place mainly due to findings of rich diamond ores and wise administration of capital by a democratic and uncorrupted government. A growing cattle industry and generous foreign aid in the form of grants, loans and expertise have also made important contributions.

However, while modern high-rise buildings are sprouting up like mushrooms in the capital Gaborone and other urban centres, and while Mercedes, Jaguars and Landcruisers are rapidly replacing the donkey carts, life in the villages and rural areas has gone largely unchanged. Certainly, there are schools and clinics and perhaps a paved road and a bus route nearby. But few rural people have electricity, which is considered too expensive even if the power lines have been extended to the village, and most of them have to carry water from a central tap, which may often run dry. Houses in the middle-sized and smaller villages are still largely of the round type with clay walls and thatched roofs, occasionally neighboured by fancier brick houses, which indicate that a family member has a well-paid job somewhere else. Although transportation facilities have improved considerably, the main movements (if any) of elderly people still go between village, cattlepost and 'lands' (agricultural fields) and quite a few have never been to one of the urban centres. Thus life in Botswana may be said to take place in two different 'worlds' between which mainly the younger people are moving.

Unemployment in the rural areas is high (21% in the country as a whole) and most young people have to migrate to the urban centres in order to find work, which is often low-paid. This migration is different from the labour migration to South Africa, which was of importance up until the 1980s, in that it equally involves young men and women. The migrating women often get pregnant and end up leaving children with their grandparents in order to continue working. Thus the villages tend to be accumulating elderly people, small children, disabled persons, unemployed and 'working failures' (people with alcohol or other kinds of problems).

One of the most important changes that has taken place in family life in Botswana is the increasing number of households with a female head (Ingstad and Saugestad 1984). This is not a recent phenomenon; we find households today that are second and even third generation female-headed. But with the advent of HIV/AIDS this is becoming more a matter of choice than before. Previously this household form was a result of widowhood (men working in dangerous occupations in mines) or of young women getting pregnant and not succeeding in securing a marriage, which they most often desired. Today more and more women, after taking the risk of having one or two children, choose to remain unmarried because they do not trust a man to be faithful and feel they will lose control of their own body and the use of condoms if they marry.

Botswana was one of the first countries in Africa to recognise publicly the danger of HIV/AIDS and to take precautions in the form of public awareness campaigns, distribution of condoms, etc. For a while they were lagging behind the countries further north in prevalence and there was hope that they might succeed in holding off the epidemic. Today, however, Botswana is one of the hardest hit countries in the world with 43% of women attending antenatal care being HIV positive and an estimate of 290,000 (out of a total population of 1.6 million) living with HIV/AIDS (UNAIDS 2002). The number of orphans is estimated at 66,000 and we may assume that most of them are being taken care of by grandparents. Today Botswana is at the beginning of a demographic transition due to the longevity of the elderly caused by improved healthcare, and a smaller number of children born to each woman. This transition is increasingly being influenced by the fact that a large proportion of the middle generation is actually dying. While the 1960s, 1970s and 1980s brought optimism and the hope of 'development', the time since then has increasingly brought sorrow and despair to many families.

METHODOLOGY

The data on which this article is based have been gathered over a period of eighteen years. The first fieldwork took place in Kweneng district

(1984–85) and was a study of family care for persons with a disability, a task in which elderly people play an important role (Ingstad 1997). The methods used were a combination of participant observation and semi-structured and informal interviews. The second fieldwork (1991–92) took place in a medium-sized village, 60 km from the capital Gaborone and focused on elderly people, both as care givers and persons in need of care, in the household (Ingstad 1997; Ingstad *et al.* 1992; Clausen *et al.* 2000). This was a multi-disciplinary teamwork combining medical examinations with semi-structured household interviews and participant observation. The team examined/interviewed all (337) people above the age of sixty in Mmankgodi. The village has been followed up with regular visits once or twice annually (the latest one in October 2002). The third study is a national survey using a structured questionnaire in combination with medical examinations (1998). This study is based on the experiences and result of the village study, intending to validate the in-depth data against data from a larger and representative sample of the population. The survey data are still under preparation and thus will only briefly be touched upon in this article.[1]

THE CHANGING VALUE OF GRANDCHILDREN[2]

When elderly Batswana talk about their children and grandchildren, they tend to do so against a background of an idealised past, a 'golden age' in which elderly people were well cared for by their well-behaved children and grandchildren. 'There are no good children nowadays' and 'there is no respect' are frequently encountered comments. However, this 'golden age'—if it ever existed—must have been placed in time well before their own generation if we are to judge from Schapera's observations from the 1930s:

> Nowadays in fact, complaints about the behaviour of the children have become very common. It is said that they are cheeky and ill mannered, showing little respect for their parents and still less for other elderly people; except when compelled, they seldom do as they are told; they take little interest in domestic work, and do not support or help their parents as they should; they have no morals in matters of sex, and their promiscuity is ruining the tribe, and filling it with bastards; they have lost all discipline and think only of their own pleasure. [Schapera 1940: 265–266]

Although we may speculate if this 'golden age' of tradition and submissive (grand)children ever existed outside the minds of elderly people, it still becomes important as a standard against which they

---

[1] I am grateful to Thomas Clausen a Ph.D. student at the University of Oslo, for giving me access to some of his yet unpublished data.

[2] Earlier versions of some of the arguments presented in this article have previously been published in Adepoju and Oppong (1994), in Ingstad and Saugestad (1984) and in Ingstad *et al.* (1992).

measure their present life situation.[3] In this idealised picture, one's own children are seen as a source of economic security and practical support. Since relatively few people in the old days lived to see their grandchildren as working adults, their role was mainly seen as the continuation of the lineage, emotional fulfilment and help with smaller daily tasks. Today things are different. Elderly people may live longer due to better health care and at the same time their responsibility for the grandchildren has increased dramatically as a result of the HIV/AIDS epidemic, which is about to wipe out a large part of the middle generation. In the national survey, 64% of the sample of elderly had grandchildren living with them.[4] In order to understand fully the changes that have taken place in the value of grandchildren we have to distinguish between the role of grandmothers and grandfathers and various categories of grandchildren respectively. As the roles of the grandmother and grandfather are very different so also are the roles of maternal and paternal grandparents.

THE VALUE OF SONS' CHILDREN

In the (idealised) traditional society, based on a patrilineal kinship system, newly married couples would settle in, or near, the compound of the groom's parents. Thus it was left to his parents to allocate according to need the money sent home from his work as migrant labourer. Several informants stated that it was often his mother who was entrusted with the money so the father would not use it on beer. One elderly lady living alone under very poor conditions with four working and married sons residing elsewhere complained bitterly: 'Before the daughter-in-law listened more to the mother-in-law than to the husband, but now she wants all the money for herself.' It seems quite possible that the desire of young wives to escape this type of control plays an important part in the decision to settle elsewhere, which is more common today. The obligation of the son to help his parents still remains, but is often not fulfilled, and the stigma of neglect seems to be fading as it becomes more common.

These changes also affect the grandparent–grandchildren relationship. Because of the traditional settlement pattern the children of sons were previously the main source of emotional and practical support for their grandparents. They would interact on a daily basis. The boys herded the family's goats and cattle, the girls helped the grandmother with the cooking, besides looking after smaller siblings, and both girls and boys helped to fetch firewood and water for the paternal grandparents. If the grandmother was widowed or unmarried the same practices would usually apply. For the first grandchild the daughter-in-law would usually go to her own mother for birth and confinement; for the following children the mother-in-law would be in charge.

------

[3] Elderly people above sixty-five years of age today receive an old age pension of 120 Pula (around £10) a month and also some support if they take care of orphans.

[4] Data from Thomas Clausen.

Through his son's children the paternal grandfather would see the continuation of the lineage and family wealth, as well as a confirmation of his own status as a soon-to-be ancestor. This too has changed, as shown by a ninety-one-year-old man, who in spite of considerable wealth was still herding his goats near the village. He had quite successfully invested money from labour migration in a grain mill and beer brewing, and used the profits for educating his sons and buying goats and cattle. However, the sons had gotten good jobs and settled in towns far away, and the grandsons were all in school. No one was interested in looking after the family's traditional capital. The man was worried about what would happen to his widow and his goats when he died and viewed his life at least partly as a failure (Bruun 2000).

We see from this case that modern education plays an important role in the changes that have taken place between the generations. This was clearly evident when we asked schoolchildren in the village to write compositions about 'How is it to be an old person in your village today?' and 'What do you think your life will be like when you grow old?' Several of the compositions portrayed old people of today as 'knowing nothing' (about modern society), and few youngsters seemed to value the wisdom of age. While the knowledge of the grandmothers concerning housekeeping, childcare, and the gathering of wild fruits and vegetables may still to some extent be valid for the grandchildren, the grandfather's expertise in keeping livestock the traditional way is becoming irrelevant.

If the paternal grandfather never married the grandmother, his relationship to the grandchildren (from both sons and daughters) would previously as well as today most often be peripheral—sometimes non-existent. This may seriously affect his chances of respect and of being taken care of in his old age, as well as of being considered one of the ancestors (*badimo*) after his death. One old man, who was quite poor, had been divorced by his wife after a short marriage and had long ago lost contact with his children and never seen the grandchildren. He was nicknamed 'Boy' by the villagers, indicating that he never really reached the status of a respected elder (Bruun 2000).

If the son was unmarried but had been living in a stable relationship, he might claim the right to his illegitimate children and let them grow up in his parents' compound. But in most cases, if the bride wealth or compensation for loss of virginity has not been paid, the son would have no rights to his children, and they would be of very little (practical) 'value' to his parents. As we shall see below, this is largely the case in current times.

Paternal grandmothers also experience changes. With daughters-in-law and their children settled elsewhere they not only lose control of the son's income, but also of the labour capacity of his family members. A paternal grandmother may no longer count on the after-school help from her sons' children in fetching water and firewood. Neither will the daughter-in-law be cooking for her unless she happens to live nearby. The important role of the paternal grandmother in caring for the newborn children of sons and their mothers while in confinement has also been weakened by the increasing number of children born out of wedlock, and the fact that an increasing number of women prefer to spend all their confinement periods with their own mother or grandmother and not with their mother-in-law—if they go into confinement at all.

THE VALUE OF DAUGHTERS' CHILDREN

Since married daughters in the old days often settled quite far away from their parents, distance could limit the contact between children and maternal grandparents. On the other hand, ties between mothers and daughters were expected to remain strong after marriage, with frequent visits by the daughter and her children to the parents' home. The daughter usually came home for delivery of the first child to stay through the three to six month confinement period. It has also been quite common for this first child, especially if it is a girl, to return to the maternal grandparents at an early age to stay and help them with daily tasks. Thus both maternal grandmother and grandfather (if married) would benefit, and the emotional tie to this child would usually be very close. Neo, a young nurse, had grown up with her maternal grandparents and felt that her grandmother was much closer to her than her own mother. When she herself bore a son out of wedlock she sent him to be fostered by her grandmother (who was by then a widow) because this was where she visited most frequently. This way she was also able to send money to her grandmother without her parents being jealous.

The present pattern of households providing for the children of unmarried daughters may be seen as an extension of the traditional practice of sending children to maternal grandmothers for fostering. The number of children living with maternal grandmothers seems to be increasing rapidly, with a maximum of fourteen in one of the households in the Mmankgodi village study, and the number may be expected to increase even more as a result of the AIDS epidemic. Many of the care-giving maternal grandmothers are themselves widows or even first or second generation unmarried mothers. For these children the grandmother usually becomes the main female figure, as in the case of Neo, the one who organises the daily life of the household, the one who makes the decisions (if there is no male head), the one to be looked up to and respected. Unmarried women living with their mothers or parents never really have the status of grown-up independent people. If they go away to work they have more autonomy, but they are still subordinate to their mother/parents when they are home visiting. With this type of relationship the grandmother/grandparents may have reason to hope that one or more of the children of unmarried daughters will eventually succeed in life and come to support them. Thus an investment in care for these grandchildren, besides being an expression of love for their daughter and her children, also becomes an investment in future security for themselves.

In this perspective it is understandable that the stigma of being an unwed mother has been fading and that some grandmothers encountered during my different fieldworks have actually been discouraging their daughters from marrying or receiving money for 'damaged' virginity or child support. Such payments could imply that rights to the child would be transferred from the family of the mother to the father and his kin. 'I love children more than money' was the answer of one unmarried mother when asked about why she had not claimed child support from the father. The meaning behind this statement is that if such support were to be given she would be afraid that the man's mother/parents and sisters would kill the child by witchcraft in order to keep him as a provider for them and the sister's children born out of wedlock.

In a previous article (Ingstad and Saugestad 1984) I have argued that we are seeing change from patrilineal and patrilocal to matrilineal and matrifocal kinship and marriage patterns in Botswana. While the patrilineal model still exists, legally and in people's minds, what we see in practice is quite different. Men have to a large extent become rather elusive characters who take more responsibility (if any) for their parents and unmarried sisters' children than for the results of their own sexual encounters. Thus their children are more likely to inherit from their mother and maternal grandmother than to get anything from the family of their father.

There is, however, a class component in this pattern. The educated, urban elite is abandoning the traditional family model for a different one in which the modern nuclear and independently living family becomes the ideal, and the relationships between grandchildren and grandparents on both sides are more equalised. Since the urban grandparents are often themselves busy workers, the mutual care and support gets tuned down and the grandparent–grandchild relationship comes to be based on love and affection alone.

The increasing importance of the maternal grandmother and the matrifocal household becomes even clearer in these days of AIDS when some women actively choose not to marry:

Mary is trained as a Family Welfare Educator.[5] She works in a clinic in one of the urban centres. Some years back she had a steady relationship with a man working in the Defence Force, with whom she had two daughters. Their plan was to get married and she had been introduced to his family. Slowly however, she realised that this man could not be trusted to 'stick to one partner'.[6] Since they were working in different towns she started to insist that he go for HIV testing before they met, but as she was starting to see AIDS patients and AIDS deaths in her job she got more and more terrified and decided to end the relationship. She did not want to marry him because she felt that by doing so she would not be able to insist on the use of condoms, and she would be even less able to control his sidesteps. For a while she would bring the children regularly to visit their paternal

---

[5] Lower-level health worker, equal to 'Village Health Worker' in many other countries.

[6] One of the slogans of the AIDS poster campaigns.

grandparents, but as the father rarely paid any support and hardly ever came to see them she stopped doing so.

Mary's mother lives in a village a few hours away by bus. She divorced her husband some years back because he also was 'running around' and 'could not be trusted'. She never sees him, nor does he give her any economic support. When Mary was having her first child she went to her mother's compound for confinement. After a few weeks, when she had to return to work, her mother insisted on keeping the baby and Mary reluctantly gave in. She could not really see how she could manage on her own with the baby and her work. When the second child was born she too remained with the maternal grandmother who is also taking care of five other grandchildren (three of them orphaned), only helped by an unmarried and unemployed daughter (the mother of the two other children). Mary would like to be with her children daily as a (modern) family and have the children feel closer to her than to her mother, but she realises the difficulties, not to mention the costs involved (paying for babysitter/maid, etc.). She is now, with her small salary, the sole provider for the large village family, a responsibility that weighs very heavily on her shoulders. Her mother asks her again and again to 'please be careful' (meaning do not take any chances with HIV/AIDS). She has a new boyfriend who comes and goes, but she insists on using condoms, does not want to marry him and does not want to take the risk of having another child (not using condoms).

The case of Mary shows clearly the shift in emphasis from the paternal grandmother/grandparents to the maternal grandmother that is taking place. This shift is accelerated by the HIV/AIDS epidemic. We see that her children are of value for her mother, not only for their love and affection, but also for the guarantee they represent for Mary's continued provisions to the household. Mary is lucky. She has a job and is able to fulfil these expectations. Many women in similar circumstances are unemployed and have to do like Mary's sister, go home with the children and work as an unpaid helper in the mother's compound. Even if they have a job they may be paid so little (for instance as maids) that there is hardly anything to bring home when the costs of living in the city have been covered. In such cases their children become an economic burden on their mother's/parents' household, more mouths to be fed and school uniforms and shoes to be bought, in addition to the costs of orphans of dying children that also have to be taken care of. The national survey shows that only 27% of the elderly who were taking care of grandchildren received any support from the parents of these children.[7]

BATSWANA GRANDPARENTS IN MORAL SPACE

Taylor is concerned with the experience of change as reflecting normative issues, not with changes in living conditions as such. In

---

[7] Data from Thomas Clausen.

Botswana, however, such a distinction is hard to make since important, and quite rapid, social changes (for instance in settlement patterns and labour migration) are closely linked to changes in what people consider moral matters (such as children born out of wedlock, and lack of support to the elderly). Thus the web of values that the elderly people find themselves in, no longer (or only partly) corresponds to that of the younger generations. One need only go back twenty to thirty years to find a situation where migrant labourers to South Africa secured their future by investing their earnings in livestock and good relations in the home village. This also contributed to a moral space for the elderly in which they were being respected and thus could experience the sense of dignity that gave meaning to their life, in spite of occasional complaints. Today the situation has changed drastically due to what is usually called 'development', and in particular the educational emphasis on individual achievement as a source of success in modern society. Thus the moral spaces of the younger generations differ in many ways drastically from that of the elderly. And even when they seek to reciprocate in ways that will please their (grand)parents there are structural hindrances (for instance unemployment and the need for rural–urban migration) which make it difficult.

In the moral space as seen by Batswana grandparents today, grandchildren may influence the three axes of moral space in different ways:

Respect
Respect in Taylor's terms has to do with what can be expected in terms of rights and duties—what the elderly as grandparents give to their grandchildren, and what they expect to receive from them. Grandparents are, as we have seen in the case of Mary, important caregivers and also a source of emotional closeness as in the case of Neo. However, seen from the grandparents' point of view, respect can mainly be measured along two dimensions: behaviour and support. As far as behaviour is concerned they would transfer the comments (above) made by Schapera about their own generation to that of their grandchildren (and children) any time. They feel that the modern school system has failed in teaching the children the manners and reverence for elderly people that formerly were taught, and even beaten into the children (especially the boys), through the old initiation rituals *bogwera* (boys) and *bojale* (girls). In the old days the grandfather would go to the cattlepost and beat the herdboys if he found them sleeping (Bruun 2000). Now, as we have seen, he cannot even get his grandsons to look after the goats because they are far away at school, and a child help-line has been put in place for children to phone if they are physically abused. The fact that some schoolchildren write in their compositions that elderly people know nothing about modern society, gives some substance to a claim of lack of respect by the elderly. On the other hand, many a schoolgirl has been ordered to move to her grandparents in the village to help them in their old age, and has done so with love and affection, although she might have found city-life a lot more

exciting. This type of support is another measure of respect as seen from the grandparents' point of view, preferably combined with the material support of the child's parent(s). When asked the question 'What is a good daughter?', one elderly lady answered, 'One that thinks about me when she eats.' This statement shows an important point; respect is not only measured by behaviour and practical help, but even more so by having a secure old age and knowing that there will be milk for the tea, flour for the porridge and perhaps some meat in the days to come.

The indications of a change from patrilineality and patrilocality to matrilineality and matrilocality that have been described here also touch upon the issue of respect. The 'disappearance' of fathers and grandfathers from daily life in many households reduces their chances of being respected by their offspring (as in the case of Mary), and the maternal granduncles cannot fill their place since they too are often elusive figures. Increased responsibility for grandchildren and household matters may increase the respect for the maternal grandmothers, but too much responsibility clearly works the other way.

Meaning

Meaning in Taylor's terms has to do with what makes a good life. Meaningful ageing is in gerontological literature often portrayed as the ability to do as many daily-life activities as possible, to take care of oneself in one's own home, play golf, travel, dance and perhaps even marry again. Batswana grandparents see this differently. Truly they appreciate being active and able to walk around in the village, to visit friends and beer-parties and participate in funerals and village meetings. But too much activity is seen as a sign of lack of help and respect from the children and grandchildren. In the study of care for disabled people in the household an elderly blind lady was being taken care of by her granddaughter in her twenties. When I tried to suggest that the lady should be taught to walk independently around the village with a cane they protested vigorously saying that this would bring shame on both her and the family. Thus we see that a meaningful life for an elderly Motswana is to be active but not too active. The grandmother should be surrounded by grandchildren, but not too many and so young that they become a burden. They should do most of the practical chores for her and she should be able to sit down and supervise it all. For the grandfather a meaningful old age is to know that he has invested his capital well, in livestock, education for children and comfortable housing. He wants to know that his sons and grandsons appreciate this and will manage the capital well when he dies. A grandfather who loses contact with his grandsons and sees his sons die from AIDS is also losing the meaning of his own life.

Dignity

Dignity in Taylor's terms has to do with honour. What are the grounds for people's claim to being honoured? From what has been said so far we see that a sense of dignity depends both on respect and on having succeeded in creating a meaningful life for oneself and the family. A man like the one called 'Boy' who has lost contact with his offspring and has no cattle or money to secure his old age, may not leave enough money behind for a proper funeral, and will not even be counted as anyone's ancestor when he dies. Thus he may socially be said to be a non-existing person, even while still alive.

A grandmother will feel that her dignity is threatened if she is locked in a never-ending carousel of caring for grandchildren and even great-grandchildren without the necessary material security and a chance someday to sit down and be cared for by others. While grandchildren previously were a source of support for the grandparents, they are becoming a burden in the time of AIDS.

On the other hand, care for grandchildren may also be a source of honour and dignity as we can see in the case of Mamodise:

Mamodise is an elderly lady, widowed a long time back and sick for many years with diabetes. Her vision has been reduced, her legs are painful and she spends most of her days lying on a mattress in the shade outside the house. Mamodise has many children, but for years she has been staying with her youngest daughter Ana. Ana is a prosperous lady. She had very little education but managed to get a steady job, although with low pay, and is involved in most issues of importance in the village. She has built a very nice house for herself and her mother, and has sent all her five children (born out of wedlock) to secondary school. She treats her mother very respectfully and always makes sure that any visitor sees her mother first. She is clearly very fond of her mother, but she is also very emphatic that she would not have been able to achieve what she has done if it had not been for the fact that her mother had cared for her children when they were babies—even to the point of letting them suckle her breast for comfort until Ana came home from work. One day, to everyone's surprise, Ana announces that she is going to get married to the father of two of her children. On being asked why, after all these years of managing so well on her own, she gives two reasons. First, she wants to honour her mother by becoming a married woman before she dies, and secondly that without being married to the father of her only daughter they will not be able to claim brideprice (*lobola*) when the daughter gets married.

Mamodise's successful claim to honour and dignity has several sources, one being the fact that she comes from a family of chiefs, another being love and affection from her children. But the fact that she has been indispensable to her daughter in building up her career as a successful village woman is probably of major importance. The daughter and grandchildren see it as their cherished duty to make sure that old granny has a life which is as good as possible, even if this means giving up some of their own individual advantages such as the free use of one's own money or the freedom of being a modern, independent woman.

Modern values in Botswana as elsewhere, tend to emphasise individual rights to self-realisation, independent living and control over one's own children and salary. This is clearly threatening for the old values on which the 'moral space' of the grandparents is founded. Ana has succeeded in making a 'career' in the village and thus was able to pursue modern and traditional values simultaneously. Thus she could keep control over her children and her income (at least up until she married) and honour her mother without her being overburdened. Mary has had no choice but to move away to find a job which she hopes is only the beginning of further training and a career within the health sector. For this she has paid the price of being distanced from her children, who consider the grandmother their main source of emotional support. At the same time her mother is in danger of being overburdened by added responsibility for orphaned and fatherless grandchildren for whom Mary is the only source of economic support. Survival has always been hard for the people living on the fringes of the Kalahari desert, but today it is hard in a new and different way, for which the elderly people are even less prepared than the younger generations. The full consequences of the combined forces of modernisation and the AIDS epidemic for the moral space of the elderly Batswana remains to be seen.

ACKNOWLEDGEMENTS

I am grateful to Alah Moyo, Harald Grimen, Susan Reynolds Whyte and Wentzel Geissler for valuable comments to this paper.

REFERENCES

Bruun, F. J. 2000. 'Identity and Social Change among Elderly Men in Rural Botswana'. Ph.D. thesis. Oslo University.

Clausen, F., E. Sandberg, B. Ingstad, and P. Hjortdahl. 2000. 'Morbidity and health care utilisation among elderly people in Mmankgodi village, Botswana', *Journal of Epidemiology and Community Health* 54 (1): 58–63.

Fossland, J., and H. Grimen. 2001. *Selvforståelse og frihet. En introduksjon til Charles Taylors filosofi*. Oslo: Universitetsforlaget.

Ingstad, B. 1994. 'The grandmother and household viability in Botswana', in A. Adepoju and C. Oppong (eds), *Gender, Work and Population in Sub-Saharan Africa*. London: James Currey, on behalf of the International Labour Office; Portsmouth NH: Heinemann.

——1997. *Community-based Rehabilitation in Botswana: the myth of the hidden disabled*. Lewiston NY: Edwin Mellen Press.

Ingstad, B., and S. Saugestad. 1984. 'Unmarried mothers in changing Tswana society: implications for household form and viability', *Forum for Utviklingsstudier* nr. 4. Oslo: Norsk Utenrikspolitisk Institutt.

Ingstad, B., F. J. Bruun, E. Sandberg, and S. Tlou. 1992. 'Care for the elderly—care by the elderly: the role of elderly women in changing Tswana society', *Journal of Cross-Cultural Gerontology* 7: 379–98.

Ingstad, B., F. J. Bruun, and S. Tlou. 1997. 'AIDS and the elderly Tswana: the concept of pollution and consequences for AIDS prevention', *Journal of Cross-Cultural Gerontology*, 12 (4): 357–372.

Schapera, I. 1940. *Married Life in an African Tribe*. London: Faber and Faber.

Taylor, C. 1985a. *Human Agency and Language (Philosophical Papers vol. 1)*. Cambridge: Cambridge University Press.

——1985b. *Philosophy and the Human Sciences (Philosopical Papers vol. 2)*. Cambridge: Cambridge University Press.

——1989. *Sources of the Self: the making of modern identity.* Cambridge: Cambridge University Press.
UNAIDS. 2002. 'Update 2002', www.unaids.org/epidemic __ update.

ABSTRACT

This article is concerned with the relationship between grandparents and grandchildren in changing Tswana society. It argues that, in order to understand this relationship and how this has been changing, we have to look at different sets of relationships separately. The relationships between grandfathers/grandmothers and grandsons/granddaughters have quite different qualities depending upon whether their sons/daughters are married or unmarried. Moreover, these qualities are influenced in different ways by changes taking place in society. The data are analysed using Charles Taylor's concept of *moral space* and discussed in terms of ideals of *respect, meaning* and *dignity.*

RÉSUMÉ

Cet article traite de la relation entre grands-parents et petits-enfants dans la société tswana en mutation. Il affirme qu'il faut, pour comprendre cette relation et son évolution, étudier séparément différents groupes de relations. Les relations entre grands-pères/grands-mères et petits-fils/petites-filles ont des qualités très différentes selon que les fils/filles sont mariés ou non-mariés. De plus, ces qualités sont influencées de différentes manières par les changements qui s'opèrent dans la société. Les données sont analysées d'après le concept d'*espace moral* de Charles Taylor et débattues en termes d'idéaux de *respect,* de *sens* et de *dignité.*

CHILDREN'S CHILDREN: TIME AND RELATEDNESS IN EASTERN UGANDA

Susan R. Whyte
Michael A. Whyte

In the evenings Rosa's kitchen was filled with more grandchildren than usual. The flickering light of the hearth played on their faces as they sat quietly watching her and the other women prepare the evening meal. The young wife of her son's son was there with her new baby. So was her daughter Maria who had left her husband to move home years ago, and whose four children were regulars among the pot watchers. The kitchen crowd had increased because Rosa's other daughter Veria had come to stay, bringing her six children, her cow and her goats. The talk was of Veria's irresponsible husband. Veria's house had fallen down completely, overwhelming evidence of her husband's neglect, and an irrefutable reason for leaving him. The husband had not returned from his last fish-trading journey to the lake months ago and Veria had heard that he was living with another woman there. Some were worried not that he was away, but that he might come home, exposing Veria to all the dangers of lakeshore sexuality. However, a few months later Veria returned to her husband's place with all but one of her children. There were whisperings that she left because of quarrels with her sister or sister-in-law. But Veria herself said that her husband's family had come to fetch them back. His parents did not want their grandchildren living 'outside'.

There are many situations like this in eastern Uganda. They raise anew old themes in the study of African kinship—lineality and relationships to children's children—themes that seem to have fresh relevance in a time of AIDS, poverty, and gender consciousness. Children's children are timely in another sense, because grandparenthood invites us to consider the temporal aspects of relatedness.

In this article we bring two analytic perspectives to bear on the 'timeliness' of grandparents and grandchildren. The first, which we call *processual time*, is the long-term, 'experience-distant', view of household developmental cycles over a historical period. Beginning with this approach, we describe the arrangements of family and marriage in Bunyole that provide the framework for people's relations to the children of their sons and of their daughters. We present material collected over thirty years that shows continuities and changes in patterns of living with grandchildren. Next we turn to the qualities and practice of relatedness, the 'experience-near' perspective that focuses on the lifeworlds of social actors. The temporality we examine here is that of

SUSAN REYNOLDS WHYTE and MICHAEL A. WHYTE teach at the Institute of Anthropology, University of Copenhagen. They have carried out field research in eastern Uganda and western Kenya on issues including kinship, health, and economic change. They collaborate with Danish and Ugandan colleagues on the long-term Tororo Community Health project.

the *intersubjective time* of shared biographies and common experience. We take the term *intersubjective* seriously, for we want to explore the ways that relations to children's children are mediated and meaningful through relations to children. From this angle, we can explore the ways in which people enact and reflect upon relatedness—producing grandparents and grandchildren through their practices.

Our interest in processual time arises in part because of our long acquaintance with Bunyole County, in eastern Uganda. We did ethnographic fieldwork there for two years starting in 1969, and have made regular return visits since 1989. Demographic material was constructed through a series of three household surveys in one neighbourhood, the last one from March 2002. Through the years we have followed changes in political economy and the consequences of the AIDS epidemic, giving us a sense of overarching historical transformations. The interest in intersubjective time comes from engagement with families we have known well enough and long enough to share memories of people and relationships. Participant observation over many years has provided one source of data for this paper. But in order to deepen our understanding of grandparenthood, we carried out a set of interviews in 2002 in our survey neighbourhood and other parts of western Bunyole with a focus on children's children. Staying with families during that month, we sharpened our senses as those relationships were played out around us.

'KINSHIP IS LIKE YOUR BUTTOCKS …

… you can't cut it off,' is the proverbial Nyole acknowledgement of the intrinsic nature of kinship. In Bunyole County, as in the rest of rural eastern Uganda, much of social and economic life is cast in the idiom of kinship. Patrilineal access to land is fundamental for agriculture, fathers are the 'owners of children' (*abeene b'abaana*) and women move to their husbands' homes at marriage. The obligation to pay bridewealth is widely recognised if not always realised promptly and fully. People position themselves in a kind of geometry of kinship, clanship and affinity as they interact with one another. When someone is introduced, his clan is mentioned. To place someone properly, you must also know the clan of his mother, his father's mother and his mother's mother. (Clans are exogamous and one should not marry into the clan of any of one's four grandparents.) The 'report' read at a burial always starts with this basic positioning of the deceased by mentioning the clans of all four grandparents. In the 2002 District Council elections, even campaign speeches at the 'rallies' began by thus properly placing the candidates. In a sense identification is placement in relation to grandparents.

A few demographic points are relevant to the practice of grand-parenting. Fertility is high and birth intervals are close: on average women bear 7.4 children in the course of their lifetimes (Kaharuza 2001). Age of marriage is lower for women than for men, especially polygynous men. So most grandparents have many grandchildren. And a woman may easily be a grandmother at the age of forty. There is a tendency for women to have a longer relationship with grandchildren than men, because they start getting children's children at a younger age.

Grandparenting is inflected by polygyny, a high divorce rate, and adult mortality. A son or daughter has children by different spouses. Grandparents split up and sometimes remarry. Grandparents and adult children are widowed and may find another mate. When a woman leaves her husband, or when he dies, or when she is sick, she often goes home to her parents or to her brothers, who usually live on their father's land (Whyte, forthcoming). She may well take her young children with her, even though there is general agreement that those children belong to their father and his family. All of these complications are part of the variety of residence arrangements that actually exists despite the widespread agreement on how people ideally should live and belong.

In a comparative African perspective, it is important to note that women are seldom recognised as household heads in this area. The few exceptions are usually widows, who are keeping the home and the land for their sons. Hardly any women own land in their own right; women are said to own houses within a compound; they are not considered to own homes. Nor is there a high level of labour migration from this district. If people migrate, they tend to buy land elsewhere and move the whole family, rather than leaving older people and children behind. Not far away in western Kenya, where we have also done research, there are many 'children of the bachelor's house', born to young women before marriage, unclaimed by any father, and left behind with maternal grandparents when their mother finally marries (Kilbride and Kilbride 1997; Cattell 1997). Although not unknown in Bunyole, this is not so common. Either the mother marries the father of her child (at least for a while), or she names the father and later sends the child to live with his family, or she takes the child with her into a marriage with someone else.

Eastern Uganda is not as prosperous or 'developed' as the central and western parts of the country. In the pre-Amin times, smallholder cotton production ensured modest cash incomes and helped to maintain what an earlier generation of anthropologists called a 'peasant mode of production'. The collapse of cotton marketing, combined with population growth and decreasing fertility of the land, have contributed to a widespread sense of impoverishment. Everything costs money today, even grass for thatching. With few dependable sources of income, and endless needs for commodities, school fees and medical expenses, Mr. Money is a constant concern. AIDS has touched every family in some way, and every neighbourhood has people with 'this disease of ours'. In this situation, everyday life is very much about mobilising and balancing resources and support, in the idiom of relatedness.

STAYING WITH CHILDREN OF SONS AND DAUGHTERS

In many ways grandparenting is symmetrical for the children of sons and of daughters. There is one word for grandchild (*omwijehulu*) and both mother's mother and father's mother are *nguhwa,* while father's father and mother's father are both *sehulu.* (The Luganda word *jaja,* meaning 'grandparent', is an endearing alternative in Bunyole.) Terminologically, there is no distinction of alternate generation relations through male and female, as there is for other kin terms. The reciprocity of intimacy, warmth, care and affection are expected between all grandparents and grandchildren. As Tolofisa, a grandmother many times over, remarked: 'Some people say that the children of your daughter are not yours, but they are all children. The children of children are yours.'

That said, the practice of patriliny and virilocality position these two kinds of grandchildren differently. The children of your married sons live in your compound, or very close by. Their presence is taken for granted. They come to play or eat, sometimes to sleep, but they run back to their parents. Daughters' children are special. They leave their father's home and move in, for shorter or longer periods. The young ones become more attached to their grandparents when their parents are not there. Some grandparents enjoy having such a devoted 'full-time' grandchild. When we asked about his daughter's children who were living with him, a grandfather explained, with a sideways glance at his wife: 'In Bunyole here, women are interested in their daughters' children.' Remembering what it was like to stay with his maternal grandparents, one man said: 'You were a new person there. The other children lived there all the time.'

Living for weeks, months or years with maternal grandparents is an old pattern in Bunyole. Today's grandparents remember it from their own childhood. To stay 'at the uncles' place' (*ebuhoja*) means literally to stay with your mother's brothers, but may actually refer to staying with one or both of your maternal grandparents who are usually living near their sons. The mobility of grandchildren is accepted even though the claims of patriliny are seldom denied. Children may have spent years with their mother's parents, but this is not usually declared a permanent arrangement. 'They might go back anytime; they'll go back when they get older; they have their owners somewhere else.' If they are boys they should go back to claim their father's land. The important difference between children of sons and daughters is that there are choices, contingencies and extenuating circumstances in the presence of daughters' children. Sons' children need no explanation; they are normally at home.

Why do grandparents keep their daughters' children? Some, like Veria's mother, do so because their daughter has left a husband who does not support them. A sick woman may come home with her small children, to be cared for by her parents and brothers. In case of death or divorce and remarriage, children are often left in the care of grandparents rather than stepmothers. Sometimes a family is too poor to support many children, or a mother has children too close together. There are a whole range of problems that explain why children are living with their mothers' parents. But sometimes a grandparent asks for a daughter's child, for help with daily chores and company. Sometimes children stay with maternal grandparents because it is closer to a school. Sometimes, people say, the children themselves decide.

Esther Goody (1982) proposed a distinction between voluntary and crisis fostering. Something of that difference is evident in Bunyole, but the distinction is not always sharp. There is a gradation in reasons for keeping a child: from sociability to convenience to alleviating a difficult situation to a dramatic event like death of a parent or being thrown out of the home. If we try to define fostering in Nyole terms, the word that comes closest is *ohuhuuma*, to 'keep or care for'. Fathers and mothers are expected to look after their children. So when we asked whether there were children being cared for in a home, there was no need to name a father's or mother's own children. Nor did sons' children merit mention if they were sleeping there, since they are supposed to live in or near their paternal grandfather's home. 'Those you care for' (*abohuumire*) are those not normally expected to be there, such as sisters' children, daughters' children, or the relatives of a wife. The children of sons or of brothers were only 'cared for' if their fathers were dead or living far away and not supporting their children. Thus one is a caretaker (*omuhuumi*) for the children of daughters, but not for the children of a son, unless he is absent.

This was the definition of fostering we used when we went back to the 'village' of Bubaali to record household composition and try to determine whether more children are being cared for today and by whom.

DEMOGRAPHIC TIME IN BUBAALI

Bubaali is a 'village'[1] which we have followed over thirty-two years. Located about fifteen minutes by bicycle from where we have stayed during many years of research, it is a place we have come to know well. In 1970 we carried out a total household survey there, combining the collection of social and demographic information with an interest in genealogy and village reproduction. We repeated the survey twenty-three years later, in 1993, and in 2002 we revisited every house in Bubaali in order to update the 1993 census, and to revisit old friends. Although Bubaali is not representative of Bunyole—much less Uganda—in any statistical sense, we felt that this case was a rare opportunity to trace the developmental cycles of households and to put some numbers on demographic patterns relevant to relations between grandparents and grandchildren.

---

[1] The term 'village' in Uganda can be ambiguous. The smallest administrative unit, the Local Council One (LC I), is usually referred to as a village. Such an administrative village may in turn be made up of two or more locally recognised villages. In Bunyole, where there is no tradition of chiefly rights over land, one or two dispersed clans commonly predominate; village leaders, called *abataka*, are selected by co-resident clansmen. Often, as in the case of Bubaali, the village name is the locative form of a clan name: BU-baali, the place of the BA-baali. Bubaali contains three groups of Babaali who are patrilineally related.

More than that, the three decades since we first surveyed Bubaali were times of historical change. Between 1970 and 1993 Uganda experienced war, civil conflict and the gradual re-establishment of civil society. It was a period of economic transformation in Bunyole. The older cotton-based agricultural economy disappeared and rice and other foods became the new cash crops. By comparison, the period 1993 to 2002 was stable. Rural real incomes—at least in eastern Uganda—have yet to reach 1970 levels but, as people say, at least there is peace. There is also AIDS, however; from the early 1990s, it was no longer a sickness of the cities. Given the reports of orphans and overstretched households in Uganda, we wondered what had happened to the pattern of caring for grandchildren in a place where we knew the situation from before.

The 2002 survey revealed population growth, as expected. But, looking at all three surveys together, we see that village household composition has changed as well. As shown in Table 1, there was a large increase in total households from 1970 to 1993; from 1993 to 2002, the number of households remains the same but their average size increases, approaching the figure for 1970. There was a fall and subsequent rise in average household size for Bubaali as a whole. Genealogical records and village history confirm that this pattern is, to a certain extent, a product of the synchronisation of the developmental cycles of households (Goody 1966) in Bubaali. Such demographic 'coordination'—which has been observed in other Nyole villages—is in turn connected to alliances and the local economic and political strategies of male household heads. It is, as Barth (1992) suggests, an 'outcome of action' and not a feature of some deeper structure of Nyole communities.

TABLE 1   *Bubaali 1970–2002: Population change*

	1970	1993	2002
Households present	29	50	50
Average household size	7.7	5.5	6.9
Total population	223	277	344
Adults	102	134	153
Children	121	143	191
Children per 100 adults	118.6	106.7	124.8

In 1970, Bubaali was a 'mature' village; a quarter of all household heads were older men (*abahulu*) with many of their married sons co-resident. By 1993, four of these men had died and their sons had become independent householders. At this point only 8% of households in Bubaali contained married sons—and two-thirds had been established after 1970. In addition, many younger sons took the break-up of the larger paternal homes and consequent division of land as an opportunity to migrate: thirteen went to Busoga where they acquired land while another nine settled elsewhere in Bunyole. Two found salaried employment in town while three more became workers (*abapakasi*) elsewhere in Bunyole.

By 2002 the pattern had changed once again. Only 34% of the households in 1993 had existed in 1970; but 74% of those present today were there in 1993. The households established by 1993 have grown both in size (from 5.5 to 6.9 inhabitants) and in complexity. Married sons are now present in 18% of households and these households represent 30.2% of the total population of the village. (At least three of the Babaali emigrants from 1970–92 have also returned and re-established households; there are also four new immigrants, none Babaali.)

What does all this mean for grandparents and grandchildren? As Table 2 shows, there was a decline in the proportion of households containing alternate generations in the 1993 survey during the period when married sons were moving out. But today the percentage has climbed back to the 1970 level. These grandparent households are where most foster-children are staying and the proportion of foster-children living with grandparents has increased noticeably.

TABLE 2   *Bubaali 1970–2002: Households with alternate generations present*

	1970	1993	2002
Alternate generation households	10	13	17
% of total households	34.5%	26.0%	34.0%
Persons living in alt. gen. households	109	93	170
% of total polulation	84.6%	33.6%	49.4%
Average size of alt. gen. households	10.9	7.2	10.0

Throughout the period, the households with fostered children were larger ones. There are no examples in Bubaali of a child sent to assist an ageing relative living alone. (The examples of smaller households with fostered children were cases where a wife's relative had come to help and where no grandparents were present.)

The number and proportion of children who were fostered went up, as shown in Table 3. Almost two thirds of these children were daughters' children. But what Table 3 also shows is that even in 1970, daughters' children comprised over half of all fostered children.

Are we dealing here with historical patterns, with different kinds of temporality, or simply with an artefact of timing? If we had merely compared 1993 to 2003, we would have had the impression of an increase in the number of grandparental households and in household size. The material from 1970, and what we know from the genealogies and family histories, suggest that there is an ebb and flow in the proportion of multi-generational households in villages at any one time. Bubaali's demography over the last thirty years surely reflects macro-events, economy and epidemiology. But it also reflects basic family developmental processes.

TABLE 3 *Bubaali 1970–2002: Foster-children*

	1970	1993	2002
Children in fosterage	19	35	52
as a % of total children	15.7%	24.5%	27.2%
Foster-children in alt. gen. households	13	23	44
as a % of foster-children	68.4%	65.7%	84.6%
Daughters' children	10	17	34
as a % of foster-children	52.6%	48.6%	65.4%
Sisters' children	3	6	2
as a % of foster-children	15.8%	17.1%	3.8%

Is there a historical transformation? The rising proportion of children being fostered, and the higher percentage of daughters' children among these, suggest that something is happening. From everything else we know, we believe that AIDS has an influence here. But fragility of marriage/partnerships, perhaps partly due to poverty, also plays a role. Looking back to 1970, we want to emphasise that, even before AIDS, people in this part of Uganda supported daughters in difficulty and cared for their children.

GRANDPARENTS AND QUALITIES OF RELATEDNESS

So far we have described forms and patterns: both the 'cultural rules' of residence and succession that Nyole people themselves emphasise, and patterns of domestic group cycles that we have registered through our household surveys. We turn now to the ways in which relatedness is talked about and enacted in daily life in order to understand the dispositions and practices that produce the patterns and processes we have been characterising.

Recent attempts to open new approaches to the study of kinship use the term relatedness as a reminder to look at a range of idioms and practices rather than taking biological connections as the most important characteristic. As Carsten (2000) summarises these approaches, emphasis is on the work of creating and re-creating relationships through everyday interactions, care and affection, cooking and eating. Relations to children's children in eastern Uganda are certainly about these kinds of practices, as we shall see. But the focus on grandchildren brings to the fore two concerns in particular: one is the linkage through another person, the mediated quality of relating to the child of a child; the other is the experience and memory of intersubjective time, time of intimacy with a grandchild and time of interlinked biographies of children, affines, and children's children. The social phenomenology of Alfred Schütz has offered general inspiration here. Although we do not employ his terminology and typologies, we appreciate his attention to the varying degrees of concreteness, directness, intimacy and intensity in relations with others, and to the temporal aspects of relations in the everyday lifeworld (Schütz 1972; Schütz and Luckmann 1973).

The mediated nature of relations to grandchildren is evident in the way people speak of connections and extensions through an intervening generation and also in the ways they contrast relations to children and to children's children. The idioms and practices we describe here are not to be understood as contingent upon relationships; not everyone talks and acts like this just because they are grandparents. Rather people give weight to these qualities when they characterise relations to grandchildren; these ways of feeling, these emphases, these kinds of practices make relationships to children's children.

Corporal connections

Kinship in eastern Uganda is not simply about biology. But careful listening reveals that Nyole people themselves invoke metaphors of bodies and biological processes when they talk about parents' parents and children's children. The word for 'parent', *omusaaye*, has its root in *ohusaala* ('to give birth to'/'to produce a child'), something both men and women do. One way of construing relatedness in everyday life is to appeal to images of concrete organs and fluids: a man 'gives a woman a pregnancy', children suck from the same breast, brothers share one blood. The 'mother who delivered me', or 'the father who produced me' is a way of describing that specific parent, among many 'parents', who provided the very womb or impregnation.[2] One man explained the difference between children and grandchildren in this corporal way: 'There is the real child who came from your body. There is also the child who came from the child you produced' (Whyte 1997: 67).

Such bodily images do not invariably carry decisive weight many years after a birth when all kinds of other qualities of relatedness have coloured interactions between people. But they are one kind of argument, as we heard in the account of the quarrel about where Perusi should be buried. She had left her husband and children many years before her death, and her father had returned the bridewealth. He wanted to bury her at his home, since she was not married and did not belong to any husband. But her sons came to beg the corpse.

> We want to bury her in our courtyard, so that some day when our children are playing and climbing on her grave, we can tell them: 'That is the grave of your grandmother Perusi, the one who gave birth to us.'

The concreteness of the grave is made to mark a physiological connection. That is one way of construing relatedness, and it worked in that case. The sons carried off the corpse for her future grandchildren. On ritual occasions they will remember her by speaking at her grave,

---

[2] In Lunyole, to make a woman pregnant is *ohumung'a ehida*, literally 'to give her a womb/stomach'.

or perhaps sprinkling beer or the blood of a chicken or goat. But the grandchildren had no direct experience of her: their interaction is with their fathers who want them to remember some*body* from whom they came into the world.

Contrasting property and affection
Where access to resources is framed in terms of patrilineal kinship, there is a discursive practice about property distribution and inheritance that invokes relatedness between father and son, brother and brother. It is not simply the case that 'rules' determine fathers' obligations and sons' rights. From a practice perspective, giving land and providing bridewealth enacts fatherhood, while receiving it gratefully shows sonship. In conflicts about resources, people invoke rules and principles as arguments to make claims convincing or to imply moral discredit. They point to the disposition of resources as the practice of relatedness. But that kind of concern characterises interactions within a generation or between fathers and sons, as Fortes (1949: 236–40) long ago pointed out. By contrast relatedness with children's children is about care, mutual help, enjoyable company, and emotional commitment. Even though most boys get a share of their paternal grandfather's land, they get it from their fathers. It is with fathers and brothers that they have property issues.

The distinction between relatedness of property and of affection/care is recognised in the appointment of two kinds of successor for a deceased man. The *omusika* ('heir') inherits the land, cattle, and wealth, as well as the obligation to pay debts and provide for sons when they grow up. An *omusika* also inherits a wife in the legal sense of taking over the rights for which the deceased paid bridewealth. The *omuhuusa* ('one who keeps/cares for') assumes the support and affection for his children, wives and other relations and the protection of their interests. When a woman dies, another woman is chosen as *omuhuusa* to replace her in relation to those who depended on her. An *omusika* is always a brother or son, but an *omuhuusa* can be a mother who takes on the care of a grandchild. The transmission of property and the extension of sympathy and care are two different ways of enacting kinship that may or may not be congruent. It is that quality of affection, free from the potential conflicts about property, that people expect and mark in relations to grandchildren.

The contrast between the tensions of property and the affection of sympathetic relations was clear on an occasion we walked into by chance one afternoon in 2002. Members of the Local Council (LC) and clan elders had been called to witness the planting of *oluhowa* bushes to mark the boundary between the land of a father and his son. This was considered shameful. Such a marked boundary should not be necessary between father and son, but there had been continual conflicts between the two even though the father had allocated land to his middle-aged son. Feelings were so strained that the son had told his children not to play in the next-door compound of their grandfather. Blame fell on the son, who was publicly reprimanded in the summing up speech of the LC chairman.

> Your father has given you land worth millions[3] ... he gave birth to you and raised you ... and also he paid bridewealth for the wife who has borne you many children... Your father has shown the heart of parenthood... Now you must accept that your children are his grandchildren. Let them come visit their grandfather and help with work and fetch water. Let them play with him and get different kinds of advice from him.

The older man had demonstrated 'the heart of parenthood' by providing for his son; in allocating resources he had performed fatherhood. Yet the son would deprive him of the company and assistance of his grandchildren, and them of the counsel he had to offer, thus inhibiting the enactment of grandfatherhood.

Intimacy and familiarity

Children are named after their grandparents, a practice that reinforces the principle of the equivalence of alternate generations. Grandparents and grandchildren playfully refer to each other as husbands and wives, co-wives or *abasang'i* ('men who have married from the same clan'). Within a family, calling a baby or an old person my husband or my wife is an expression of affection that often evokes a smile. This kind of playfulness takes place in other situations too, for the relationship of grandparent is categorical. Members of your father's mother's and your mother's mother's clans are all grandparents; teasing and joking about marriage relationships (*ohuduha enganda*) is good sport. Cleverly done, it is the source of much amusement when 'grandparents' and 'grandchildren' meet on the path or at a gathering.

The intimacy and ease with grandparents contrasts with the correctness and modesty that people express in relations to parents (a category that includes aunts and uncles) and parents-in-law (especially those of the opposite sex). Sexual modesty (*obuhwe*) discourages adult 'parents' and 'children' from touching, sharing clothes, entering one another's sleeping space, or talking about matters construed as sexual. But children of all ages sleep with their grandparents. As girls get older they unroll a papyrus mat in the house or kitchen of a grandmother at night. Boys build a bachelor's house (*esiimba*) close to the house of their grandparents, so that when they bring girls, they can do so discreetly in relation to their parents.

Parents of both sexes show affection to small children, holding them and carrying them. But grandparents are especially close physically; 'to lean on granny' (*ohwediha hujaja*) is a habit of grandchildren. Sitting talking to grandmothers and grandfathers, we often noticed their children's children hanging onto them, sitting on their laps, being patted affectionately. 'A good grandmother or grandfather carries you like an

---

[3] In 2002, one US dollar was worth about 1,800 Uganda shillings.

egg,' explained Flora. 'They reserve special treats for you, like dry meat, smoked mushrooms and white ants.' Many people say that grandparents are too affectionate. They do not discipline their grandchildren; they spoil them. At your grandparents, you enjoy freedom (*eryana*). Some grandparents agreed: 'How can I beat my husband?' 'Let their parents discipline them.' Others proudly said that they insisted on rules and proper behaviour, and were ready to use the stick. Several remarked that modern educated parents did not want their children to live with grandparents because they would get spoiled and stupid.

INTERSUBJECTIVE TIME AND CHILDREN'S CHILDREN

Historical time, even the developmental cycles of homes and villages experienced over a lifetime, is not of immediate concern to people in Bunyole. Most of our interlocutors did not generalise about a radical transformation in family life brought about by AIDS, for example. If asked whether life has changed, most older people say yes, but the abstract view of history and family is not very relevant to the practicalities of their everyday lives and relationships. Rather they are concerned about particular persons in configurations of people with whom they have shared time and experience, and with (or without) whom they imagine possible futures. This intersubjective time is sometimes recounted as a story that gives meaning to the present situation. Sometimes it is evident in the way people seem to be considering who will assist whom in the future. Attending to this sense of time with other people can help us to understand the motivations, feel for options, and actions that produce overall patterns of continuity and change. The quality of 'time together' was evident in the way effort and familiarity were assumed to lend depth and intensity to relationships with children's children. The best examples were the dyadic face-to-face (body-to-body) interaction of grandmothers with their small grandchildren over months and years. Intersubjective time has another aspect, however, when parents invoke the biographies of their children in relating to their grandchildren. Here they are not relating dyadically to individuals, but to social persons in a web of interlinked histories of partly overlapping experiences.

Grandparents struggle for their grandchildren. A grandfather should go to divine the sickness of his grandchild, a grandmother should nurse the patient. Both should use every means to mobilise resources when their grandchild is in need. A neighbour woman came to beg money to buy medicine for her son's child. She had spent long nights in vigil over him at the hospital, but his life was hanging on a thread. 'I wouldn't ask for myself,' she said, 'but it's my grandchild.' When the mama in the family where we stay went to mourn her in-law, she wanted to spend the night there, but decided to come home the same day because her malnourished great-grandson would cry all night without her. Although not all grandparents invest such effort and sacrifice in their grandchildren, doing it or remarking on having done it creates a sense of a particular kind of relatedness.

Nawire felt it would be hard to take her first son away from his grandmother where he was staying. 'He really disturbed (*ohusumbuha*) her, when I got pregnant with the next one.' The history of having been bothered, of going through difficulties, was part of their bond. One woman explained that women love children more than men because they suffer (*ohubonabona*) with them. It is not simply that you struggle because you love, but you love because you have struggled. Many grandparents spoke of how they had worried and exerted themselves when their grandchildren were sick, as if that explained why they were so close to them. Why should Sunday's grandmother feed and sleep with his child, when he was living right next door with his wife and another child? Because she had stayed with that child in hospital and nursed him through a terrible illness. (Several people remarked that she had done the same for Sunday when he was a child and that was why she loved him so much.)

A history of having spent time together is an important quality of a relationship. People remarked about this especially in connection with children and their grandmothers. The Lunyole verb *ohunala* means 'to become accustomed to', 'to be familiar with'. When children 'overstay' with their grandparents, they get used to them and do not want to leave. When we asked further about the child Nawire left with her mother-in-law, she said that the child had grown accustomed. The grandmother had cared for him from early in his life, because the next baby arrived very soon, and now the child was used to his *jaja*. 'His heart is for his grandmother' (*Gali n'omwoyo gwa nguhwawe*).

Children extend relationships to their parents. That is to say, there is a sense in which they represent their parents—the past, present and future with them. In Lunyole, a child is sometimes referred to as the branch (*olusaga*) of the parents. Caring for someone's child has implications for relations to that someone. This is the point of much literature about fosterage, of course; ties are strengthened through the exchange of children—caring for a child shows you care about its parent. One grandmother in Bubaali explained that she had taken a child from each of her daughters, so as not to favour one more than the other. It is also the point, in an interesting twist, of Bledsoe's work (1990, 1995) on children of previous unions in Sierra Leone. She shows that the treatment of stepchildren depends on relations between a couple; because children are identified with their parents (including the ex-spouse), they become tokens in the relationship with a new spouse. For that reason, children of previous unions are often sent to stay with a grandparent, rather than expose them to mistreatment by a step-parent.

In relation to grandparents and intersubjective time, this point helps us to understand two recurring interrelated themes in the stories people told about why they were caring for their daughters' children. The first was sympathy with their daughter; the second was criticism of her husband and in-laws. There were many examples of daughters like Veria, who were neglected by their husbands, or widowed and pushed out by their in-laws. Often grandparents told about how they had lived through the difficulties of their daughter's marital problems from their own position and were bitter about the in-laws' behaviour. The tone of indignation was unmistakable as they told why they were caring for their grandchildren.

Salimati Kadondi interrupted cutting her grandchild's hair to tell us about the three daughter's children who were staying with her.

> My daughter's husband deceived her saying they should work together to grow rice and get money to build a house. Instead he used the money to bring another wife. That woman used medicine to change his mind. He lost interest in my daughter and her children. For four years, my daughter would come home here and then go back, always hoping that her husband would change. Finally she gave up. The last child was born here [she nods at the three year old sitting on her lap and snuggling cosily against her]. I myself took the grandchildren to their father's home to mourn when their paternal grandfather died. But their father, my son-in-law, didn't bother to help his children, even when he saw them. He's just there with his other wife.

This story could as well have come from 1970 as from 2002. As we saw in the survey material from Bubaali, people have been taking in their daughters and daughters' children for a long time. The grounds given for doing so, then as now, are often the failings of in-laws. The evidence is taken from past experience, your own and that of your daughter. Expectations about the future are based on these experiences. If they did not treat your daughter well, they are not likely to treat her children well, especially if there is a new wife in the picture.

Accounts of experiences are of course told in relation to given situations in the present. When Veria came to her mama's with all her children, the talk was about the failings of her husband who allowed her house to fall down. But when his family came to take them back, people spoke of their good heartedness, their affection for Veria, and the future land prospects of her sons, a point to which we shall return in a moment.

What has changed since 1970 is the frequency with which daughters come home because they are ill. It has long been the case that women with chronic conditions, mental illness for example, often went back to their parents and brothers for care. With the advent of AIDS many daughters come home sick bringing their children, sometimes after their husbands have died. The pattern of criticising the in-laws for heartlessness and neglect is common in these cases. It is not only the illness that is the problem; it is the way the husband's family acted.

Alupakusadi has two daughters at home with their children. One is a widow, who is ill herself; she has five children with her. The other left three children with her former husband, and brought two with her. (She has 'the sickness of not eating salt' so she cooks in her own kitchen.) 'It's all on my head [to care for them],' he says. His eldest daughter Sabesi sits outside plaiting mat strips and tending her sick baby, while he chats with us and family members in his son's house.

> When Sabesi's husband died, his family did not suggest an heir to be her new husband, because of the sickness. In fact, they didn't care. They have

bad hearts. Two and a half weeks after the funeral, they brought her and the children here in a car. There was no help there. One child remained behind at her dead father's home. She was just wearing a rag. She was pulling grass to get money for a dress, but her stepmother took the money. Finally I went and got that grandchild too; I bought her a dress to put on before bringing her here.

Alupakusadi's account is about his bad-hearted in-laws as much as his grandchildren. We do not know their side of the story. Maybe they thought Sabesi would be best cared for by her own mother; maybe coming home was Sabesi's own choice. Perhaps the children wanted to come with their mother. But Alupakusadi's story put the blame on them, and justified that his daughter's children were with him rather than with 'their owners', their father's people.

One of the things that strikes us from following Bubaali over three decades is the persistence of patrilineal rights to land. How does that fit with all those daughter's children taking refuge from bad-hearted in-laws? In spite of the hard words about in-laws, most grandparents said that their grandsons would go back to their father's home to claim their land when they grew up. 'The children of owners cannot remain,' remarked one grandmother, even as she expressed hope that her sick daughter's two sons would come to stay with her. By pointing out that their patrilineal connection was elsewhere, she was asserting their future claims to land. 'I am just a keeper (*omuhuumi*),' said another, implying a distinction between affectionate caring and property relations. There is a delicate balance between criticising the in-laws and supporting a grandson's possibilities for the future.

These considerations about the future probably explain something else that came out of the Bubaali survey. Of the children being cared for, there were half again as many girls as boys. There seems to be a tendency to leave daughters' sons in their fathers' homes if possible. Alupakusadi's other daughter had brought two daughters home, and left two sons and another daughter. And he asserted firmly that Sabesi's son would go to his father's people when he got a little older. It is because of the future that sons' sons and daughters' sons are different. Granddaughters are expected to marry and move to their husbands, so they are more similar. For boys, links of patrifiliation are paramount.

There is one more point from the survey material that bears exemplification in connection with intersubjective experience. It was evident that the households with grandparents caring for daughters' children were large ones. Although this was not invariably the case, it seems that homes with more social resources may attract foster-children. Instead of seeing grandparents as a passive 'dumping ground' overwhelmed by burdens of care, we had the impression of many as active and resourceful. They were nodes in networks, participants in family arenas, rather than individual older people alone with their burdens. The following notes from a visit to a neighbour illustrate the way that daughters' children fit into a family history and a set of social resources.

When Lucy explained about the orphans (*abalehwa*) of her daughter living with her, she told about their father who never came to see his baby when it was sick: 'I got tired of writing letters to him about his child's illness. Those many worries are what gave me [high blood] pressure.' The baby died and so did Lucy's daughter. Lucy brings a big brown envelope with X-rays of her daughter's lungs (tuberculosis was reported), receipts for medicine, and slips with lab results, together with photos of various family members, a copy of Lucy's son's driving licence, and her husband's voter registration. In this 'family archive' is the evidence of how she managed to get her daughter to Mulago Hospital with help from a grandson who works for an Indian in Kampala. 'But after all that,' she sighs, 'they said this isn't the type of sickness that can be operated.' Lucy's daughter Esuka joins the conversation. She had helped to care for her sister and now shares a house next to her parents with the two orphans and three of her own children. (The other two are with their father, or rather in a room he rented for them at the trading centre, since his new wife did not want to care for them.) It is a large and orderly compound. Lucy and her husband had nine children. Besides the house of Esuka and those grandchildren, there are those of a son and his two wives and children. At lunchtime, all these children flock to Lucy's kitchen in their school uniforms. Two children of her brother are among them; they live too far from school to go home for lunch. We offer Lucy a little money as mourning (*esiho*) for her daughter (we had not been there since her death five months earlier) and Esuka takes us to see the new grave at the edge of the compound. We notice that it is the only one that is cemented.

Depending on how we interpret 'the sickness that cannot be operated', Lucy may be a grandmother caring for AIDS orphans. But she is not a hapless victim of historical forces. Like other grandparents who have lost their married daughters, she was most concerned about the immediate history of her relations with her neglectful son-in-law and with others from whom she might mobilise help. Her efforts and their assistance had secured X-rays and a cement grave. Her daughter's children were not just living with their grandmother, but with their grandmother's people. In fact Lucy was one of the few who did not envision sending her daughter's son back to his father. 'If God helps us, we'll buy him a plot. When he grows up, we'll help him,' she said.

In a sense, our examples of invoking interlinked biographies and shared experiences complement Carsten's analysis (1995) of the politics of forgetting on the Malaysian island of Langkawi. She argues that forgetting details about the lives of grandparents who immigrated to the island from many different backgrounds allows the construction of a common present. 'The enormous emphasis on the production of children in marriage and the image of the community as one of shared grandchildren are both aspects of this forward projection' (*op. cit.*: 326). Instead of 'looking downward' towards shared grandchildren who will create ties in the future, the Nyole grandparents who spoke to us of their daughters' children were remembering events in the past that divided them from their daughters' affines. But our point is that 'micro-politics' can be glimpsed here as well: there is a situational pragmatics in remembering and forgetting. Grandparents who in one context remember ill-treatment of their daughter at the hands of her husband's family may still put that memory aside in another when their daughter's son goes back to his paternal home to claim land from his father.

CONCLUSION

Analytical assumptions about time have very different implications for understanding relations between grandparents and grandchildren. Structural processes of generations succeeding one another and developmental cycles based on the bio-time of fertility, growth and ageing have the virtue of reminding us that not all processes are unidirectional and progressive; there are cycles and repetitions. Historical time in the sense of a narrative of processes of change can easily become hegemonic with its focus and plot. It can oversimplify and ignore both continuity and variation. In the concern with the social consequences of AIDS, for example, it is easy to overlook all the other reasons why children may be staying with their grandparents. Still, our research would be myopic and less interesting without tying it to some larger story about what is happening in the world.

Intersubjective time is our term for the experience of time with other people, typically acknowledged in the recounting of who did what, and how that relates to where I am now. These are not 'life stories' but remarks or reminders about shared experience and connections to other people. They are situated in a more immediate way than dominant historical narratives. While history 'unfolds', intersubjective time is contextual and contingent, relative to purposes, positions and strategies in a field of other subjects. It is socially creative, placing events (divorce, illness) within a weft of remembering that can guide action and affection, justify a situation, or keep future possibilities open. For relations between alternate generations, this kind of temporal perspective is important because it makes us see individual grandparents as subjects interacting with other subjects, not only grandchildren, but also adult children and in-laws. These interactions produce the patterns that we as ethnographers describe in more distant or abstract terms as processes.

ACKNOWLEDGEMENTS

We would like to acknowledge the support and collaboration of the Tororo Community Health (TORCH) Project and our colleagues at the Child Health and Development Centre, Makerere University. The Danish International Development Agency has funded our cooperation for the last nine years. Fred Luhonda helped us with the most recent survey in Bubaali and with interviews of his neighbours there. Special thanks to the families of Antonio Guloba and the late Tefiro Wamudanya for sharing time over the years. Erdmute Alber and Wenzel Geissler provided helpful comments on an earlier draft of this paper and Karen Fog Olwig made suggestions about relatedness.

REFERENCES

Barth, F. 1992. 'Towards greater naturalism in conceptualizing societies', in A. Kuper (ed.), *Conceptualizing Society*. London and New York: Routledge.

Bledsoe, C. 1990. 'Differential care of children of previous unions within Mende households in Sierra Leone', in J. Caldwell, S. Findley, P. Caldwell, G. Santow, W. Cosford, J. Braid, and D. Broers-Freeman (eds), *What We Know about Health Transition: the cultural, social and behavioural determinants of health.* Vol. 2. Canberra: Australian National University.

——1995. 'Marginal members: children of previous unions in Mende households in Sierra Leone', in S. Greenhalgh (ed.), *Situating Fertility: anthropology and demographic inquiry.* Cambridge and New York: Cambridge University Press.

Carsten, J. 1995. 'The politics of forgetting: migration, kinship and memory on the periphery of the southeast Asian state', *Journal of the Royal Anthropological Institute* 1 (2): 317–35.

——2000. 'Introduction: cultures of relatedness', in J. Carsten (ed.), *Cultures of Relatedness: new approaches to the study of kinship.* Cambridge and New York: Cambridge University Press.

Cattell, M. G. 1997. 'The discourse of neglect: family support for the elderly in Samia', in T. S. Weisner, C. Bradley, and P. L. Kilbride (eds), *African Families and the Crisis of Social Change.* Westport CT: Bergin & Garvey.

Fortes, M. 1949. *The Web of Kinship among the Tallensi: the second part of an analysis of the social structure of a Trans-Volta tribe.* London: Oxford University Press, for the International African Institute.

Goody, E. 1982. *Parenthood and Social Reproduction: fostering and occupational roles in West Africa.* Cambridge and New York: Cambridge University Press.

Goody, J. (ed.). 1966. *The Developmental Cycle in Domestic Groups.* Cambridge: Cambridge University Press.

Kaharuza, F. 2001. 'Short Interpregnancy Intervals and Child Survival'. Ph.D. Thesis. Faculty of Health Sciences, University of Aarhus.

Kilbride, P. L., and J. C. Kilbride. 1997. 'Stigma, role overload, and delocalization among contemporary Kenyan women', in T. S. Weisner, C. Bradley, and P. L. Kilbride (eds), *African Families and the Crisis of Social Change.* Westport CT: Bergen & Garvey.

Sangree, W. 1997. 'Pronatalism and the elderly in Tiriki, Kenya', in T. S. Weisner, C. Bradley, and P. L. Kilbride (eds), *African Families and the Crisis of Social Change.* Westport CT: Bergin & Garvey.

Schütz, A. 1972. *The Phenomenology of the Social World.* Trans. by G. Walsh and F. Lehnert. London: Heinemann. (1932. *Der sinnhafte Aufbau des sozialen Welt. Eine Einleitung in die verstehende Soziologie.* Wien: Springer.)

Schütz, A. and T. Luckmann. 1973. *The Structures of the Life-World.* Vol. 1. Trans. by R. M. Zaner and H. T. Engelhardt, Jr. Evanston IL: Northwestern University Press. ([1975]. *Die Strukturen der Lebenswelt.* Neuwied: Luchterhand.)

Whyte, S. R. 1997. *Questioning Misfortune: the pragmatics of uncertainty in eastern Uganda.* Cambridge: Cambridge University Press.

——forthcoming. 'Going home? Burial and belonging in the era of AIDS', *Africa.*

ABSTRACT

This article brings two analytic perspectives to bear on temporal aspects of relations to children's children. The first, which we call *processual time,* is the long-term, 'experience-distant', view of household developmental cycles over a historical period. Beginning with this approach, we describe the arrangements of family and marriage that provide the framework for people's relations to the children of their sons and of their daughters in Bunyole County, eastern Uganda. Household survey material collected over thirty years in one village shows an increase in the number of grandchildren being cared for, as expected in an era when parents are dying of AIDS. However, it also qualifies the hegemonic historical narrative of AIDS by showing that other factors have been and still are at work in influencing the patterns of caring for grandchildren. The second analytical perspective is that of the *intersubjective time* of shared biographies and common experience. The emphasis here is on the 'experience-near' qualities and practice of relatedness as they are lived and talked about in the lifeworlds of social actors. They are evident in the dyadic relations between grandparents and grandchildren and also in the ways that these relations are embedded in other connections to children and in-laws. When grandparents take on the care of a daughter's children, they are mindful of the past, present and future of her relation to her husband and his family. The concept of 'intersubjective time' points to the intertwining of the lives of three generations and provides a rich complement to the more abstract concern with developmental cycles and historical processes.

RÉSUMÉ

Cet article se sert de deux perspectives analytiques pour étudier les aspects temporels des relations avec les enfants d'enfants. La première, appelée *temps processuel*, est la perspective à long terme, «éloignée de l'expérience», des cycles de développement des ménages sur une période historique. Cette première approche décrit l'organisation familiale et conjugale qui forme le cadre des relations entre les personnes et les enfants de leurs fils et de leurs filles dans le comté de Bunyole, dans l'est de l'Ouganda. Les données collectées pendant trente ans dans un village dans le cadre d'une étude sur les ménages montrent une augmentation du nombre de petits-enfants pris en charge par leurs grands-parents, comme on peut s'y attendre à une époque où les parents meurent du SIDA. Cependant, elles tempèrent également le narratif historique hégémonique du SIDA en montrant que d'autres facteurs ont joué et jouent toujours un rôle d'influence sur les schémas de prise en charge des petits-enfants. La seconde perspective analytique est celle du *temps intersubjectif* des biographies partagées et de l'expérience commune. L'accent est mis ici sur les qualités et la pratique de la parenté «proches de l'expérience» telles qu'elles sont vécues et discutées dans l'univers de vie des acteurs sociaux. Elles se manifestent dans les relations dyadiques entre grands-parents et petits-enfants, ainsi que dans la façon dont ces relations s'inscrivent dans d'autres rapports aux enfants et à la belle-famille. Lorsque les grands-parents prennent en charge les enfants de leur fille, ils ont à l'esprit le passé, le présent et le futur de la relation de leur fille avec son époux et la famille de celui-ci. Le concept de «temps intersubjectif» désigne l'entrelacement des vies de trois générations et fournit un riche complément à la question plus abstraite des cycles de développement et processus historiques.

SHARED LIVES: EXPLORING PRACTICES OF AMITY BETWEEN GRANDMOTHERS AND GRANDCHILDREN IN WESTERN KENYA

P. Wenzel Geissler
Ruth J. Prince

Classic social anthropological studies on kinship in Africa made important observations about the relationship between alternate generations, grandparents and grandchildren. Radcliffe-Brown (1940, 1949) described the 'friendly equality' and 'permitted disrespect' in what he categorised as a 'mild joking' relationship and linked these traits to a 'cyclical' understanding of life and time, in which children and the elderly share a life outside the sexual stage of life, close to the invisible world of the ancestors' spirits.[1] Fortes' observed how Tallensi grandparents 'spoil their grandchildren', because they regard them as their living link to the future (1949: 236–40) and noted the importance of this for children's education, the formation of personhood and the reproduction of sociality (1938). Both Radcliffe-Brown and Fortes seem to find pleasure in observing these relationships on the margins of their structural-functionalist frame. It is this particular pleasure deriving from practices of amity that this essay tries to explore further.[2]

This paper is based on fieldwork in a village that we will call Uhero, in western Kenya, between 1996 and 2002.[3] After some general reflections about Luo grandmotherhood and a brief overview of the lives of grandparents in Uhero, we shall examine three rather different grandmothers in western Kenya at the turn of the twentieth century, and look more closely at two areas of formative practice that have been

Having read Human Science and Medical Anthropology, RUTH PRINCE worked on several health-related anthropological research projects in Kenya before embarking on her Ph.D. at the Institute of Anthropology, University of Copenhagen, and the Danish Bilharziasis Laboratory. WENZEL GEISSLER received his Ph.D. from the Faculty of Natural Sciences, University of Copenhagen, based on health research conducted with the Danish Bilharziasis Laboratory in Kenya. He subsequently studied social anthropology at Cambridge University, and now teaches social anthropology at the London School of Hygiene and Tropical Medicine, University of London.

[1] Radcliffe-Brown's observation of 'disrespect' was shaped by Western notions of respect and authority and underrated the different, not necessarily hierarchical, construction of 'respect' in many non-Western societies where respect may well be associated with equality and where it is respect, rather than its absence, that underlies and enables licence and intimacy between grandparents and grandchildren (see, for example, Serpell 1993: 31–59; Van der Geest 1997a: 21; and, for the Luo, Grigorenko *et al.* 1999).

[2] The general traits of the grandparent–grandchild relationship (privileged familiarity, role-joking and nicknaming, sharing, mutual care and reciprocity) have been described for various other African societies (e.g. Kidd 1906 [Zulu]; Raum 1940: 156 [Chaga]; Turner 1955; 1996: 244–257 [Ndembu]; Erny 1981 [Kongo and other groups]; Brindley 1986a, 1986b [Zulu]; Blacking 1990 [Venda]; Serpell 1993 [Chewa]; Lancy 1996 [Kpelle]; Reynolds 1986, 1996 [Shona]; Whyte 1997 [Bunyole]; Heald 1999 [Bugisu]).

[3] All names of places and persons have been replaced with pseudonyms.

described as central to the relationship of amity between grandmothers
and grandchildren in the literature cited above: naming and addressing,
and material giving and sharing. Naming is a responsibility of the old
people of a home, and playful address, nicknaming and role-joking is
particularly salient between grandmothers and children. Sharing (in
play, domestic production and consumption, and in bodily care) is
central in the everyday life of children and grandmothers. Both naming
and sharing constitute relatedness through acts of everyday practice,
and, we shall argue, should be understood in relation to each other;
both make, in different ways, the other part of one self and create shared
substance; yet the relations they produce are momentary and have to
be sustained in continuous shared life. Whilst naming and sharing are
part of the everyday practice of those who live in Uhero, and practices
of amity or *hera* are important aspects of all social as well as kinship
relations, we chose to focus on these practices as they play out mainly
between grandmothers and grandchildren. Theirs is the most 'free' and
unrestricted kinship relation in Luo society, the relation that for many
Luo embodies *hera*.

We focus on naming and sharing not as timeless social practices but
because they are contested and negotiated, opening up debates among
villagers about the practice of amity in social life. Naming and sharing are
considered crucial to the child's social becoming, the formation of her
person. Variations and contradictions in these forms of childcare reveal
different available imaginations of personhood and sociality in Uhero.
For *JoUhero* ('the people of Uhero'), children and grandchildren are the
centre of life and caring for them is the ultimate aim of most everyday
activities. However, for different people and in different situations,
good childcare may be different, depending on expectations of what
a child should become and what an adult can and should do towards
this. Different ways of caring for children point towards different
concepts of the person and relatedness. Some practices emphasise the
creation of relations, which transform the status and existence of all
involved persons, their relations to other people and things. As the child
grows, these practices continuously make and remake the person. Other
practices aim (often explicitly) at furthering the child's development into
a supposedly autonomous subject through processes of accumulation
and ordering, strengthening the becoming person's boundaries and
capacities, making a complete, individual self. These different practices
and ideas of how one can and should bring up children are not
separate cultural forms but coexist and engage with each other in Uhero,
although villagers and ethnographers alike may occasionally label them
as 'western' and 'Luo', or 'modern' and 'traditional' as if they belonged
to different places, people or times. In everyday life, they are not cast
as coherent, contrasting ideologies of nurture (such as 'individualist
vs. relational') that are adhered to as wholes by different people or
families, but they are variously called upon in different situations—even
by the same people—and provoke debates, dilemmas and creative
compromises. We argue below that although many grandmothers tend
towards interactions with their grandchildren that emphasise relatedness

over autonomy, they have to find their ways between the different practices (and values) that coexist in present Luo sociality.

GRANDMOTHERHOOD

During our fieldwork, the children's bond with grandmothers appeared more affectionate and embedded in joint daily life than the bond with grandfathers. Historical descriptions of Luo social life also emphasise the central role of old women for childcare and instruction (Evans-Pritchard 1965; Hauge 1974; Cohen 1985; Otiende *et al.* 1992: 7 ff.). Why would old women be more prominent in their grandchildren's lives than old men? There are practical reasons for this gender difference in rural Luo society: children's needs are socially constructed as female, domestic activities, and it is domestic and agricultural work done by women that children mainly participate in. Boys learn male work, like herding, from peers and fathers rather than grandfathers, and the economic importance of these male activities has diminished over the past century in favour of wage-labour, whereas female activities have retained their vital importance. Moreover, there are demographic reasons for the greater prominence of old women. In many African societies, including Kenya, more women reach old age than men do (Apt 1996: 10); the marriage age is lower for women than for men (Potash 1978); and the practice of polygyny means that children commonly have one grandfather in the home they live in, but several and younger grandmothers. Hence, for a child the likelihood of living with a grandmother is greater than that of living with the grandfather.

Most importantly, grandparenthood is not simply defined by generational position, but shaped socially in relation to gender. A woman's adult life consists of two different life-ages: as wife and mother she is at the centre of production and reproduction but has initially little authority in the home; as mother-in-law and grandmother, she gradually moves out of the sexually reproductive core of the family but enjoys increasing authority and personal freedom (see James 1978). Only women experience this marked transition from the social status of a wife into a grandmother, from adult to old woman (Mead 1967; Potash 1986; Holy 1990; Whyte 1990; Holmes and Holmes 1995). Men in principle never reach this peripheral position relative to the (sexually) reproductive core of the domestic group. *JoUhero* see reproductive sexuality as a powerful and potentially dangerous practice, and children are protected from contact with the sexuality of senior kin by social rules sanctioned by a serious illness, *chira* (see Parkin 1978: 149–163; Abe 1981). As long is she is sexually active, a woman cannot 'hold' (*tingo*) a grandchild 'across her lap' (*riwo*), which effectively prevents nursing care such as treating, feeding, and sleeping with a child. Once she is 'old'/'big' (*duong*) she is permitted to hold grandchildren.[4] Many

---

[4] Rules like this and others, such as the one prohibiting sexually active women from preparing medicines for young children, protect the vulnerable child from the powers of

women adhere to this rule and some women choose to redefine their sexual status in order to be able to care for a grandchild, such as happened in the case of Atieno, who was born while her mother was still in teacher training college. Although still of reproductive age, Atieno's maternal grandmother decided to abstain from sexual contact with her husband and thus to 'become old', so that she could take care of her granddaughter. Irrespective of when in life she becomes 'old' and whether she chooses to be so or not, if a woman lives long enough, she has a post-sexual or post-reproductive period, during which she can live closely with grandchildren. In contrast, men can (imagine to) sire children up to their death and should therefore not be physically close to their grandchildren. Even though a man is old in years and a generational grandfather, his post-reproductive age is not socially recognised and he does not become a social grandfather in the same way that an old woman does.

Imaginations of the Luo grandmother

For many Luo, grandmothers represent tender memories of the past: the time of their childhood and the time before they were born, which the grandmothers embodied and taught them about.[5] Compared to the present predicament of Luo society, particularly the suffering brought by AIDS, this past appears to many people, irrespective of their age, as a better time. The imagination of the Luo grandmother in literary writing (e.g. Ogot 1966: 2; Odinga 1967: 7–10; Ogola 1994) and scholarly accounts (Ominde 1952; Onyango-Ogutu and Roscoe 1974: 24–32; Ocholla-Ayayo 1976; Cohen 1985) is tied to the institution of the *siwindhe*, the large, round, grass-thatched house where, until one or two generations ago, children slept with an old (classificatory) grandmother, who then was referred to as *pim*.[6] In such accounts, Luo grandmothers epitomise the past, a lost world. A few novels, such as Oludhe MacGoye's *Victoria* (1993) and some recent research on the social consequences of AIDS-related death in western Kenya (Nyambedha 2000) show that Luo grandmothers are more than icons of a lost world and are not only objects, as well as producers, of nostalgic accounts. Using their experience and status, grandmothers negotiate new ways of life, new bonds between a past that is not all passed, a

---

sexual contact: the sanction against 'holding the child' is concerned with the thighs and the lap of the woman, the term *riwo* designates acts that merge and share substance, such as commensality or bodily love, and the rule is sanctioned by *chira*, the illness that results from wrong kinds of physical, particularly sexual, touch.

[5] As Proust's figure of the grandmother as embodiment of past virtues illustrates, this topos is of course not limited to contemporary Luo, but it gains salience and popularity at times when historical change is experienced as loss and decline.

[6] The term *pim* is rarely known by contemporary Luo youths, while the term *siwindhe* is commonly used as the embodiment of past life and values and the cradle of 'Luo culture'. For example, the question, why girls get pregnant so early nowadays may provoke the answer: 'Because today we have no *siwindhe*'.

present that continuously brings new challenges, and a future of which they know as little as their grandchildren.

The lives of grandmothers in Uhero
In 2001, Uhero had 914 inhabitants distributed across ninety-nine scattered patrilineal, virilocal homesteads. With few exceptions, people engaged in subsistence agriculture, some planted locally marketed cash crops, some of the men fished and both men and women engaged in short-distance fish trade. Many of the older people (that is, over fifty years of age) had lived and worked in towns before settling in their rural homes, and many of Uhero's young people were moving between village and town, working or looking for work. Most households relied for their cash needs such as schooling and medical care on the remittances of these migrants. Out of the total population, 40% were fifteen years of age and below, 12% fifty years and above, and 48% between sixteen and forty-nine years of age. This age-distribution probably shows the mark of AIDS, the middle age groups being reduced by the many deaths among younger adults.[7] AIDS (or *ayaki*) was rarely mentioned in relation to specific deaths, but there was a general recognition of what was called 'the death (*tho*) of today', which many saw as but the pointed edge of a general situation of loss and decline captured in the common expression among old and young: 'The land (*piny*, also 'earth' and 'community') is dying.'

Among the villagers of fifty years of age and above, sixty-eight were women (forty-six of them widows living on their own) and forty-eight were men (only one of them being a lone widower). Elderly *JoUhero* had to shoulder an increasing burden of care for grandchildren, including obligations such as school fees, and they increasingly cared also for daughters' children or grandchildren outside their patrilineal obligations, who stayed with them as their parents had died (see Nyambedha 2000).[8] Almost all elderly women in Uhero lived with grandchildren and most children lived or had lived with a grandmother. Customary habits prevent children from sleeping in the same house as their parents; instead, girls should sleep in the grandmother's house until they move out of the home, ideally to get married, and boys should do so up to adolescence, when they build their own hut, or go to sleep with age mates or in a neighbouring home (see Mboya 1983; Ominde 1952; Ocholla-Ayayo 1976; Cohen and Atieno-Odhiambo 1989). Despite people's varying attitudes to 'tradition', these habits continued to shape

---

[7] During our last year of fieldwork, forty-two deaths occurred in the village: only ten were old people above fifty years of age; eleven were young children under five; and twenty-one were adults.

[8] As Luo society is patrilineal, sons' children belong to the home, while daughters' children cannot normally be given land in their maternal grandparent's home. However, they often end up staying in the maternal grandmother's home because grandmothers have a close relation to their daughters and their children. Several grandmothers in Uhero have thus accommodated daughters' sons, and some have even allowed them to build a house (referred to as 'kitchen for the boys', since daughters' sons must not build a 'house').

residential patterns. Some children slept in the grandmother's house whilst eating with their mothers; others, especially those whose mothers were living elsewhere or had died, lived entirely with their grandmother.

Different grandmothers in Uhero lived very different lives. The three grandmothers we present below: Maria (b.1920), Mercy (b.1950) and Magdalene (b.1955), lived on their own with their grandchildren, but their wealth, livelihood, everyday life, education and residence were rather different.[9] Despite these differences, they represented more fortunate grandmothers. Others were less lucky. Maria's older co-wife Akech (b.1915), who had been 'inherited' by their late husband, died of neglect and starvation in her hut, only a hundred yards from Maria's house and Maria's son's home, which were full of grandchildren. Maria's neighbour Veronica (b.1915) had lost six of her seven sons during the previous decade and had begun to bury her daughters-in-law and her adult grandchildren, whom she lived with in a large empty home. The sons of Jane (b.1925) had died too and although she was lucky to live with her daughter, granddaughter and great-granddaughter (an unusual uterine residential group in this virilocal society) they had no wage earner in the family. These less fortunate grandmothers remind us that many elderly women lived alone with grandchildren because their children had died and many were in a precarious position. Some, like Maria, praised themselves for being blessed with children and grandchildren, but others suffered.

Intertwined lives
The lives of grandmothers and grandchildren that we observed were marked by physical nearness and intimacy: sleeping and sitting closely, sharing food and talking and touching each other in gestures of tenderness such as arranging a dress or removing an insect. This sense of pleasant conviviality was expressed in the twenty-eight compositions that the older pupils of the village school (aged sixteen to nineteen years) wrote about their grandmothers (most of them about co-resident paternal grandmothers). Although several complained about moody and quarrelsome or even cursing grandmothers, none mentioned physical punishments by grandmothers and several described how the grandmother protected them from their parents' ire. In the two cases in which the grandmother was described as mean, the authors contrasted this to expected grandmaternal behaviour. All of them constructed their accounts around complementary everyday activities—planting, harvesting, bringing water and firewood, shopping, grinding—leading up to joint cooking and eating of food, which a large proportion of the compositions dwelled upon. The youths emphasised that their grandmother 'always gives when asked', 'always shares her food', and 'welcomes me', particularly with 'sweet' foods such as potatoes, curdled milk or porridge and vegetables cooked with milk. All mentioned the

---

[9] Years of birth were estimated in five year intervals for people aged 50 years and above.

stories, songs and riddles the grandmother would tell, and while some of this might be evocations of stereotypes, the compositions' details of sitting together, telling each other stories, praying, extinguishing the light and falling asleep convey the youths' appreciation of their grandmothers' care, which in many accounts extended to the payment of school fees and medical expenses.[10]

The youths conveyed their feeling of nearness with the grandmother in statements such as: 'we love each other', 'she does anything for me and I do anything for her', 'she is always happy with me', 'she listens to our words', 'I tell her if I have trouble', 'she calls me sweet names', and 'she praises me'. Many referred to the fact that they owed their own life to the grandmother: 'she gave birth to my father', 'I was born in her home', or 'she is the reason why I am here'. The compositions often took a funny, tongue-in-cheek tone, describing for example the old lady's unpredictable moods as 'caterpillar's transformations', or praising the grandmother as 'a mother who spoils me'. Accounts of conflicts showed that, if grandmother became too much, one could withdraw, and unlike in conflicts with parents, one could answer back and have arguments, and one could even, after a quarrel, forgive her, and agree again, underlining a much greater degree of mutuality and liberty than in parent–child relations.

TWO GRANDMOTHERS

Maria (b.1920)

Let us begin with the woman in Uhero who in her daily life and in her own view comes closest to the idealised Luo grandmother of the past: Maria, and her granddaughter Susanna (b.1982). We met Susanna when she was eleven years old and a bright pupil in the local primary school. When we showed interest in her knowledge of herbal medicines, she took us to her grandmother Maria's house to learn about Luo herbs (see Prince *et al.* 2001; Geissler *et al.* 2002). Here we found a situation of privileged familiarity that evoked classic Africanist ethnography: Susanna slept with numerous other grandchildren in Maria's small house, the remnant of her grandfather's once large homestead that lay behind her parents' home. The children supplied the old lady with lake water and firewood and shared, often from one plate, the food Maria produced in her gardens. Their conversations were peppered with jokes and teasing. Maria addressed Susanna as 'co-wife' and Wenzel as classificatory grandson and thus their shared 'husband', and complained that Susanna was taking too large a share of Wenzel's attention. We understood little then of the sexual implications of these jokes and relational addresses, which played on intergenerational equivalence and on relations that these references opened up.

---

[10] All but one child also mentioned that the grandmother had given or even taught him or her about herbal medicines.

Maria and her grandchildren were in constant physical contact, cuddling, holding hands or tidying each other's hair or dress, sitting or lying beside each other and chatting. Maria called these small, intimate everyday practices (sharing food, tenderness, work, talk and jokes) 'love' (*hera*). Susanna's interest in her grandmother's stories and medicines was an expression of that love, as was Maria's readiness to provide and share food, or to divulge to her knowledge that she would not have shared with her daughters or daughters-in-law (see Prince and Geissler 2001). Amity, intimacy within productive work and commensality characterised everyday practices around Maria's house. When asked to explain 'love', Maria would say 'we are together' (*wariwore* or *wabed kanyakla achiel*) or gently shake a hand that rested in hers, or she would point at the child at her feet, eating from her bowl, or at one coming with water or firewood from the lake. For her, the children's contributions to their joint household, like the gestures of bodily closeness, materialised the bond between them.

The children who lived with Maria were her son's children and his grandchildren, from his sons and daughters. Irrespective of their genealogical ties, they shared Maria's sleeping mats, food, and the work around the house. Despite patrilineal ideology and virilocal residence these relations were not contingent upon lineage or biological kinship; instead closer bonds, such as between Maria and Susanna, arose from daily practices and shared presence and they were open to change. As a teenager Susanna enjoyed the grandmother's leniency, and her boyfriends, or so Maria claimed, appreciated Maria's kindness with small gifts of tobacco. In 1997, Susanna dropped out of school. She was sent by her mother to stay with distant relatives in town and on her rare visits home Maria complained: 'My co-wife from town can no longer sit down in her clean clothes.' Susanna became an example of the youths' lack of love. Less than a year later, whilst working as a maid in town, Susanna became very sick. She was hospitalised on a psychiatric ward and later treated by a healing church. Some said that a co-wife of her mother had sent spirits (*jochiende*). Others suspected that Maria's ancestral spirits (*juogi*), which had troubled Maria during the same period and made her wander through the bush at night, had also affected Susanna, underlining the lasting affinity between the two. Two years later, when Susanna was married and living in Kisumu town with her husband, she resumed her regular visits to the grandmother, bringing sugar, soap and tobacco, receiving herbal treatments for various complaints and instructions about pregnancy and birth, pleasing Maria with small acts of tenderness and sleeping in Maria's house again. Recently Susanna gave birth to a son. Playing on their 'co-wifely' relation, Maria addressed Susanna's son as 'my son' and during Susanna's visits home she advised her young 'co-wife' on how to care for him.

Occasionally, Maria complained about the changing ways of life compared to her own childhood in her grandmother's house. Like many other elderly women in Uhero, she stressed the present-day lack of food and its implications for the grandmotherly relation: 'if there is no food, there is no love'. Milk used to be the main source of fat in the past and a fluid with genealogical connotations; old people had many cows, and the downward flow of milk within the homestead was the embodiment of the grandmaternal relation linked to shared meals, time, talk and learning. Today, cows are few and milk is often sold. Since commensality is the substantial basis of relatedness in Uhero, Maria complained: 'How can I stay well with these children if I cannot eat with them?' In Maria's view, money was also a problem: the boys sold fish instead of bringing it to their parents and grandparents, and the girls diverted their attention to these fishing boys. Resources that in Maria's view should have been shared around her house were diverted elsewhere, and a form of vital closeness and shared substance was lost. Emerging class differences, greed and imaginations of social mobility—epitomised in money—were driving a wedge between people and generations: 'These days, if you have no money, you have nothing,' Maria would say, or: 'Where there is money, there is no love.' This did not mean that Maria did not appreciate some money from grandchildren and others, but she feared the social differentiation that, in her experience, money could sustain.

Maria blamed school for the lack of helping hands in the garden and complained, like many old people, that school children had little 'respect' (*luor*) and became 'proud' (*sungore*), superior towards older, uneducated people.[11] Despite these misgivings, Maria sold land and cattle to pay her older grandsons' secondary school-fees; without her, few of the children would have finished primary school. Maria was not the only old woman in Uhero who experienced this dilemma of schooling: she regretted that the role of the *pim* (the classificatory grandmother of the old days who lived with and taught the children of her lineage) was eroded by school, but she accepted school as part of her responsibility for the children's education. Maria's problems with growing economic disparities, money and schooling were brought together in another favourite topic of her diatribes, 'Saved' Christians (*jolendo*, 'clean people' [born-again, mostly Anglican Christians]) who, in Maria's experience, strove for social distinction and had little respect for the 'old ways' (see Cattell 1992).

Mercy (b.1950)

One of these Saved Christians was Mercy, the late parish priest's widow and hardworking nurse in the local health centre, who lived with her grandson Dadi, born in 1996. Theirs was a different kind of home from Maria's: a modern stone house, in which family members had separate

---

[11] 'Respect' is a key to social relations in Uhero and to evaluations of social change. The meaning of the Luo term is wider than the English equivalent and closely related to 'love' (*hera*) (Grigorenko *et al.* 2001). It emphasises mutuality which is underlined by traditional Luo tales. In one, a grandmother shows disrespect for the granddaughter who cares for her, peeing on the fire and a'sking her to get new fire from the hyena, who eventually eats the old lady; in another one, a grandson is rendered mute after greedily eating the grandmother's food, showing lack of respect by rejecting commensality (Onyango-Ogutu and Roscoe 1974: 50, 67).

rooms, and in which the Luo rules of avoidance, such as the prohibition against parents and children sleeping under one roof, were considered to be un-Christian and mostly disregarded. Dadi was the first child of Mercy's oldest son. He lived with his grandmother because his father worked in town. Dadi was born two years before the grandfather died and was named after him. Around the time when his grandfather died, he began to speak and learned to pronounce his full name 'Reverend Doctor John Ogumba', which he was regularly asked to perform for visitors. While his grandmother called him 'Dadi' (the 'father' of the home, that is, her late husband), others addressed him jokingly as 'head of the home', 'son of Alego' (where his grandfather was born) or as '*padri*' (Swahili: 'priest').

In Mercy's home, Dadi was the only child of her own children. Mercy introduced the other children whom she had in her care as 'orphans' (though, in classificatory terms they were children and grandchildren). Helping in the household, they lived a different life from Dadi, who was also distinguished from them in dress and food. He took his supper beside the grandmother on the sofa and had his own little plastic chair to sit in the garden. At night he slept in the grandmother's bed, while the others slept in the living room. During the day, since his grandmother worked in her clinic, Dadi was lonely. His relation to the children who helped in the house was a little tense, and his grandmother did not wish to have neighbours' children in the home or Dadi to visit them. She was worried about dirt and infections, but also about her property and Dadi's small possessions. Like food and sweets, toys were shared between children in the village with little consideration of ownership. When we followed a wire-model of our Land-Rover (hoping eventually to appropriate it) it reappeared in several different homesteads, passed from the older children who made it to the younger ones, until it eventually disintegrated. Such movement becomes a problem if the toys were bought from scarce resources, such as Dadi's battery-driven cars, his first prestigious properties.

Mercy hoped to send Dadi to the same private nursery school in Kisumu that his father had attended. As Mercy once said about Dadi and our son, ingenuously merging affection with economic, educational and medical concerns: 'They are class A children, PhDs, we must keep infection away from them.' The other children in the home attended the local school, where Mercy paid their uniforms and fees. Although such differentiation between children was disapproved of by Maria and other villagers, school fees force one to differentiate between the children one is responsible for, to focus on one's 'own' children. Together with the emphasis on the nuclear family and narrow biological kinship in Anglican ideology, schooling reproduced class-patterns (between 'grandson-and-heir' and 'poor relations') inside the home.

Dadi's privileged, protected loneliness and the high expectations placed on him, seem very different from Susanna's life (and that of the twenty or so other grandchildren in Maria's home), but as with all imaginations of difference, fieldwork leads one from moments where these are clear to moments when one's eye catches commonalities.

Mercy was physically very close to Dadi: she ate with him, bathed him and slept in one bed with him. Occasionally she remarked that he ought to sleep alone in his bed, as his fathers had done when they were small, 'to become self-disciplined', but then she admitted: 'Without him, I feel lost. I mostly talk to him, even during the night.' The bedroom, the double bed under the mosquito net that Dadi and his grandmother shared, was part of another way of life from that of the children on Maria's reed mats on the mud floor. But tenderness and intimacy were important in both these grandmothers' lives. Before we present a third grandmother, we want to look more closely at the differences and commonalities by examining the practices of address and of sharing, formative social practices that are important in the lives of all grandchildren and grandmothers in Uhero.

ADDRESS

The attribution, to every individual, of an unequivocal personal, proper name is a 'strategic' practice in de Certeau's sense (1984: 34), closely associated with a specific subjectivity and particular practice of ownership. A person owns her name together with her personal properties, and the name serves as legal referent for material, private possessions. In contrast, everyday address is a universal human practice that arises from specific moments of encounter. It is literally a 'tactical' practice, situated *between* one and other, moving towards the other; an act of touch, not attached to one person; a shared moment. As such, practices of address have a potential, behind their playfulness, to challenge the economy of bounded persons and properties, which the modern imagination proposes as an ideal to people in Uhero and elsewhere.

Names

ID cards and school registers in Uhero often contain a Christian name, a Luo name and a family name. The latter is supposed the equivalent of Western surnames, but most people use their father's Luo first name and these names may change between generations. Elite families, like the Reverend's, carry a lasting family name (often that of the man who received baptism, education or political office and 'founded' the family and its assets). An important complement to these names are titles such as 'Reverend' or 'Dr' that underscore an understanding of the person as a product of hard work, self-development and accumulation, through which capacities are added to the self. While family names and titles emphasise the boundaries of the person, the family and their assets, 'Christian' names such as Mandela, Rambo, Clinton or Cinderella allow for more creative choices and innovative connections.

The Luo name in official documents and everyday use is usually a common Luo name given in relation to the circumstances of the birth, such as Ochieng' ('boy born during mid-day') or Adhiambo ('girl born in the evening') (Ocholla-Ayayo 1976: 182–184). Only rarely is it the name of a dead ancestor (*nying' juogi*), which relates the child to a deceased relative, and which should be given by a grandparent (*-chako*, 'to name after', 'to initiate'). *Juogi* are the spirits of one's 'old people' (*jomadongo*) or 'grandparents' (*kwechewa*) who protect the well-being of their descendents. *Nying' juogi* points towards the vulnerable core of a person because they reveal the living human's relation to a dead one, to whom she owes some of her life-force. They are powerful not as markers of the individual identity or self, but as vital references to others and to the bonds that preceded the existence of the person. Therefore these names provide a key to the bearer's life and well-being: if one wants to harm somebody through sorcery one needs to 'know him' (his real name and his ancestors). Hence many people hide the *nying' juogi* from outsiders or in official contexts and often only the older people of one's family know one's *nying' juogi*.

Ideas and practices about *juogi* are a key to people's different orientations towards past and modernity. When asked what *juogi* means, old Maria, feigning innocence, began: '*Juogi?* That is how we call our children.' She went on, however, to demonstrate how *juogi* 'smack their lips when they eat with us at a funeral', where they must be given a share in the meal because 'they are our people'. In contrast, Mercy said: 'They are devils, like witchcraft' and clarified, somewhat ambiguously: 'We do not believe in them, but some people in this village do bad things with them.' For Saved Christians like her, acts that refer to or get in touch with *juogi* equal 'backsliding' into a heathen past. These diverging connotations of *juogi* influence the use of names. Some parents try to avoid contact with ancestors by naming children after living relatives, especially if they become dedicated Christians, or after the death of other children has been attributed to an ancestor's interference. Thus Susanna and her four younger siblings, born after the death of several baby boys, were not named after *juogi*, while the older eight children all carried such names. However parents may change their minds, for example if an illness is traced to an offended ancestor who demands to be placated by naming the child after him.

Children are not named after a *juogi* immediately and often their names change during their first years of life. To name, one must 'know the child': identify similarities of body, face or character with particular dead people. Only when one knows 'who she is' can the right name be given. If a child is given the wrong name, the person whom the child was not named after may bring illness. If this cannot be solved by the old people of the home addressing the child with alternative names until she becomes well, divination (nowadays often done by one of the independent African churches) is required. Another reason for the fluidity of children's names lies in practices of concealment. Names may be hidden from other relatives or outsiders because they refer to old conflicts and may endanger the child's well-being, or simply because the mother wants to appear Christian in one context and committed to the 'old people' in another. Even adults are often referred to by different Christian or Luo names by people who got to know them at different times or places of their lives.

Some 'modern' educated people reject the possibility of another person living in the child, which would contradict their Christian faith and the supposed autonomy of the person. Apologetically, they reduce the name of a dead person to a symbol: 'We just do this to remember.' Others explain the meaning of *nying' juogi* as pre-Christian belief in reincarnation. In their effort to explain the practice unequivocally, neither appreciates the metonymical function of these names. Such names create neither identity with another person nor a mere mental referent for the other, but bring different persons (and embodied by them, time past and time future) in touch with each other. This touch has concrete effects: a child embodies physical traits of the deceased and resembles him in character; the body of the child rejects the same food items that were prohibited to the deceased, underlining the dimension of bodily oneness that the names of *juogi* entail (individual 'food prohibit...' linked to specific ancestors are very common in western K........ child may share her namesake's capacities and deficienci........h ..s why one should not name a child after a relative who died childless. Moreover, the child shares the deceased's relations with living and dead people. Names of *juogi* produce continuity between living and dead persons and thereby also among the living. These are relations of substantial, embodied sharing, but they do not create an 'identity' as such; they are not exclusive, but tie one to other people and merge one into these. In Lienhardt's term they 'interfuse' one and other (1985: 154).

Addresses

In everyday interactions, people call (*-luonge*) each other by kinship addresses such as 'our mother' (*minwa*), 'mother of...' (*Min...*) or 'daughter of...' (*Nya...*) (see Waligorski, 1968) or use praise-names (*-pake*) and nicknames (*-ngere*) (see Ocholla-Ayayo 1976). In relations that demand respect, to call someone by her name (*-luonge nying'e*) is rude, like 'calling somebody names'; 'she never called me my name!' praises a respectful person. Calling a person by her name is at the same time too distancing (individuating and thus negating the web of relations that link one to the other) and too personal (touching upon a vulnerable core of personhood). If one calls somebody by her proper name instead of a relational address, she could retort, 'Do you not know me?' since only the person-in-relation is a person, while the separate individual is, in a sense, unknown. Official visits, for example between in-laws, centre around formal introductions in which one explains one's relations until everybody knows how to address one. Relational addresses belong to and define particular relations and do not, like proper names, belong to the one addressed. They involve a third party, underscoring that relations are not mere connections between two individual subjects but between the relations that constitute them as persons.

Kinship teasing—particularly grandmothers' play on the intergenerational equivalence of alternate generations—allows for entertaining play with sexual connotations, and rehearses kin-relations, rules, manners

and what to expect of social life (see Blount 1971: 29). Such practices give room for inversions of hierarchy and contestation: Maria's
five-year-old grandson Moses was praised as a 'good husband' when
he brought Maria a fish the big boys had given him, but sometimes he
turned away her wifely affection and told her to 'look for the husband
in the grave' beside the house. The relations that playful addresses
create are not restricted to ancestors but can produce wider connections, creating, for example, ties between small boys and great men:
another grandson, little self-confident Nelson Mandela was commonly
likened to his great namesake, 'Mandiba, who answered back, too'.
This produces polyvalent and ambiguous chains of relations, which are
evoked in everyday conversation, recreating memories of dead people
of the past and directing children towards their future lives. Mandela's
ten-year-old sister, Juma, was praised for her (not yet existing) feminine
shape and beauty, referring to the beautiful relative who lent her the
name; from there the talk went to that relative and back to Juma, scru-
tinising similarities of their character and cautioning Juma to become
'good like her aunt'. Like many villagers, her mother stressed the link
between address and moral education: 'If you are called somebody
good, it makes you struggle to become like him.' On the one hand, you
are the other; you owe your life and your characteristic traits to him and
therefore are called after him; on the other hand, names and addresses
(and not only the *juogi* reference) oblige you to emulate the namesakes,
to become like them.

The play with relational addresses and the multiple narrative
connections it establishes can transcend the realm of kinship and
contribute, along with other practices, to the inclusion of non-kin
friends into domestic patterns of relatedness: Little Ingeborg, Maria's
youngest granddaughter, was named after our classificatory mother (an
aunt from Germany), who had spent much time smoking together with
Maria, and happened to leave Uhero on the day Ingeborg was born.
Ingeborg's mother called the child 'Mother of Wenzel'. When Ingeborg
peed on Wenzel, her mother commented that 'your mother, the one
who carried you and suffered, greets her son', and told him to appreciate
his 'mother's gift'.[12] Juma, Ingeborg's sister, cheekily demanded respect
from Ruth, as she too was now Ruth's classificatory mother-in-law, and
she reminded the baby to cover herself properly, recalling Ingeborg's
namesake's often too casual dress. Ingeborg's father called her jokingly
'Sista' ('nurse') referring to the professional future of this 'white lady'.
Neighbours remarked on the imagined whiteness of her skin. Old Maria
reminded her to 'bring tobacco' and gave Ingeborg's mother herbal
medicines to ensure the well-being of her 'friend' (see Prince *et al.*
2002). Ingeborg was not yet one year old when she was surrounded

---

[12] This interpretation of an infant's peeing resembles the meaning that is given in Rwanda
to the child's first faeces in the ritual meal 'to eat the child's excrement' (Taylor 1992: 69).
The first bodily fluids are here regarded as primary social acts that establish relations through
sharing substance (see below).

by this play with addresses. As she grows older, more references will accumulate in the different ways she is called, and as long as Maria, her grandmother, lives, they will have a special relation in which the pleasures of tobacco will figure prominently.

As this naming-play concerned a Christian name and a non-kin namesake, the jokes are light-hearted. If these addresses refer to kin and ancestors, more is at stake and more complex webs of relations can be spun, weaving living and dead, absent and present people into the child's life. The examples show how relational addresses evoke both particular qualities of the namesake, that are recognised in the child or which the child is admonished to strive after, and multiple intergenerational relations, that the link between child and namesake fosters. The result of this everyday address is not an unequivocal personal identity, but fluidity and ambiguity. The contradictions and paradoxes of this play give pleasure and remind us of the malleability of relations and of our selves in these. The references to dead or absent people are not lasting attributes nor 'incarnations', they are neither metaphors of, nor monuments to, dead persons, but fleeting references, some out of a momentary situation, some lasting for a while, others again changing as the child grows up. Their use allows for playful and instructive evocation of rules of respect and of familiar experiences—like that of jealousy of co-wives or conflicts between husband and wife. And through them, invisible people with more or less substantial ties to those interacting are made present in everyday talk and take part in concrete everyday life. In this play, a person is continuously refashioned through references to bodily and psychological traits, memories and narratives of other persons and relations. Addressing not only creates a composite person, one composed of others, but her composition is continuously re-created. She is not the 'additive' product of the 'properties' of mother, father, ancestor, etc., but continuously merged and made between others. Between the physically grounded kin-address 'mother', which implies owing one's existence to the other, and fleeting joking addresses like 'white lady' to a black infant, lies a continuum of addresses that evoke others' contribution to one's self. Working metonymically these addressing practices create zones of overlap, which configure the person in everyday practice.

A significant exception to the practices of name-avoidance and relational address in Uhero are members of the wealthier Anglican families. Like Mercy, they prefer calling each other by the Christian first name or family name (and title) and avoid *nying' juogi* or nicknames, except for praisenames that stress economic and educational achievement. While these different practices of naming and address do evoke different ideas about the person and social relations, nobody in the village can avoid relational address. Even if one prefers one's surname and title, most people address one relationally and many social situations demand such address. Moreover, relational address can well be employed in a condescending manner and thereby stress, against its original purpose, social difference. One can shift creatively between the registers: somebody may introduce a visitor as '*Daktari*' (Swahili:

'doctor'), yet call him 'my son', emphasising both social status and close relatedness.

Like Susanna's brothers, little Dadi was nicknamed with reference to his grandfather, and he called Mercy accordingly 'Darling'. However, the particular play with his 'proper' name—proudly enunciating the grandfather's titles 'Rev. Dr ...' in front of people with no such education—underlined his singularity and his family's achievements, rather than obscuring his individuality and entangling him in relations with others. It had more the character of a monument, a fixed marker of memory, than of the fleeting metonymical evocation of the past that relational address can achieve. Ancestral spirits, which Maria accepted as part of life, were anathema here: grandfather 'went to heaven' and did not live as a spirit in the little boy. But then again, this may have been so for his grandmother, but for other people the dead priest's name nevertheless evoked ancestral associations.

SHARING

Naming and addressing children are modes of sharing relations and material and immaterial aspects of the person, acknowledging that one owes one's life to others. In domestic life, they are tied in with practices of giving and sharing things. In the past, when a newborn was taken out of the house, libations were given to the name-giving ancestor. If it was found that a woman's difficulties in conceiving could be traced to the intervention of an offended ancestor, a chicken was offered to the ancestor and dedicated to the not yet conceived child, who was given the ancestor's name. The chicken was kept and bred in the home as living embodiment of the tie between ancestral force and unborn child (see Mboya 1983: 117–8). Even today, if a child's sickness is attributed to an offended ancestor, offerings are made such as spilling a chicken's blood in the child's *juogi* name. More commonplace tokens of relatedness are the small chickens maternal grandmothers and namesakes give to small children to raise. Nowadays such customs also incorporate commodities: a good Christian name-sake ought to provide the essential goods of motherhood required for baptism and hospital-visits (dress, nappy, towel, soap and baby powder). As noted above, the little child returns these gestures: he 'greets' the grandmother or other persons who hold him with his urine, the first substance he can give and share. According to Maria, in the past the newborn child was laid on the ground outside the house on the day it was 'taken out' (*golo nyathi oko*) and greeted by people, and left until it urinated.[13]

---

[13] See also note 12. Past Luo rituals around taking the child out of the house included giving the child herbal medicines and fermented porridge (Mboya 1983: 92), which possibly induced defecation (as most Luo remedies do), suggesting a similar emphasis on the first giving.

The first address

Sharing things with others, a highly valued social practice, begins in a child's life with a particular form of address. One of the first words a toddler in Uhero learns is *miya* ('give me'). This is provoked by others, who address her when she holds something, saying: *miya, miya!* expecting her to give the object and returning it to her afterwards. Rarely do children deny this request. In his studies of early language development, Blount (1971: 13) observed that the second word a Luo child learns after *mama* is *miya*, learned from adults' requests to younger infants to give them objects they hold and thereby to 'entice them into an interaction frame' (*op. cit.*: 6). This first dialogue contrasts somewhat with our son's first exchanges with age mates on a Danish beach, turning around the possessive pronoun 'mine'. Without making claims about first words in different societies it seems as if different people and different material conditions encourage a child to engage in one or the other sort of primary communicative event. 'Mine' and *miya* link self, other and a thing in specific ways: one lays claims to ownership and presupposes the existence of an owning subject; the other one puts a request to the other, prior to and constitutive of the emergence of the person.

Abel, the old village jester, who called us his grandchildren, taught us how important this 'play' is when, over a drink on our veranda, he half-jokingly drew Wenzel into an argument about giving him his shoes. Wenzel defended his property, explaining that they were dear to him, that he had no money to buy new ones, etc., but the point that Abel made, that he could glimpse a second pair of shoes behind the door while he himself had bare feet, forced Wenzel in the end to give him the shoes. Abel took them as they had been given, with both hands like a gift. Then he spat a blessing over them, laughed, and gave them back, praising a white man's ability to learn.

Sharing is important in social life: children in the village often played sharing imagined or real food, and food items or toys given to one would be shared out among those present. Their parents and grandparents gave large shares of their scarce food to visitors and neighbours and to people they went to visit; not being able to welcome others to share food was a main concern during times of drought. Of course, the other's call to share is not automatically heeded. At times, the one who asks, the matter asked for, or one's plans make one avoid giving. But if people who have food in the house refuse to share without a reason, they are judged mean. A good reason, such as expecting visitors, is acceptable, but it is the one who has something but refuses to give who must prove his needs, and not the one who comes to ask for something. The other's demand has priority over ownership.

Sharing is probably an educational aim, if not necessarily the foremost, in many societies and across different educational ideologies. Some parents and grandparents (Sister Mercy as well as ourselves) try to foster 'altruism' in children by a moral argument: 'This is *your* thing, *but* you should share, because if you give (some of) it to the one who doesn't have, you are a *good* person.' Here, giving is a moral obligation that arises from one's prior claims to property—the owning subject is beyond doubt. Altruism differentiates, makes the other in the act of giving. We think *miya*-playing exemplifies another approach, beginning with the address 'give me', learned as soon as the child can hold a thing. 'Give me' are the first words of the other, which cannot be rejected as it is through others, and through these words, that one becomes somebody. These contrasting educational practices point, we think, to an important difference between amity and altruism, and between sharing and exchange.

When the child grows older, the demand *miya* is controlled by pride and courtesy, but it remains embodied in the face and regard of the other person. Whether said or unspoken, encounters remain ideally shaped by the first words of the other: 'give me', to which one responds with the thing at hand (in Uhero it is usually food) and with words, looks, touch and gestures. This suggests a 'passivic' axiom of sociality in Emmanuel Lévinas' sense (e.g. 1985: 76) according to which it is the primary event of the other's request upon me that makes me a person. It could be differentiated from an 'agentic' view of social practice, in which the inter-action with another person is imagined as intentional acts of subjects: 'I am, this is my thing, let us exchange'. The point here is not to oppose, say, 'Western' and 'Luo' personhood and relatedness. Rather, *miya*-playing suggests a 'passivic' way of imagining sociality, which is as universal as is today the fiction of the autonomous agent.

Sharing or exchange?
The object that is asked for in *miya*-playing is irrelevant, and the other person's call (and not one's ownership in a thing) is the primary social fact, upon which give-and-take follow. The play draws attention to a relation that is prior to discourse, interaction prior to, and giving rise to, personhood. This is better understood as 'sharing' (contact-through-a-thing, with the implication of consubstantiality) than as a form of economic 'exchange' (thing-obtained-through-contact, with the implication of return), as a communion rather than communication. The stress adults put on this play suggests that what is rehearsed here is a basic pattern of practice regarding others and things, in which the transaction as an encounter foregoes the objects of exchange and the exchanging subjects. This transactional mode differs from economic exchanges of objects between acting subjects, in which objects (often commodities) are given and received by subjects as individual properties.[14]

---

[14] Transacted in this way, objects carry a different value from the one that stems from their production or exchange. While the latter is imagined as inherent to the object, this other value derives from the moment—the movement of giving it to the other. This notion of value without locus, duration and measure of equivalence underlies many material transactions in everyday social life in Uhero. And again, the same applies elsewhere, but often its specificity is overshadowed by dominant models of exchange. Maybe this value suited a sociality where few objects had intrinsic, measurable value outside the relations in which they were made

Sharing and its distinctiveness from exchange (Woodburn 1998) has been discussed in hunter–gatherer studies (see Wenzel *et al.* 2000), which suggested that our (Western) 'proclivity to find exchanges' (Hunt 2000: 19) makes us assume underlying reciprocity and thereby assimilate sharing into an economic logic of return. This prevents us from recognising that sharing is firstly about the production of relatedness (e.g. Bodenhorn 2000) and persons (e.g. Macdonald 2000) and only secondarily about distribution or transaction of objects. Rather than being confined to hunter–gatherers, sharing is a possibility of human social practice alongside exchange; it is not a primordial survival but a universal possibility (Bodenhorn 2000).[15] Sharing among Luo and others deserves more extensive scrutiny. Here, we limit ourselves to its role in the grandmaternal relation, because the distinction between sharing and exchange influences how we imagine the conflation of tenderness, bodily care and talk, productive work and consumption that were salient in the lives of Maria and her grandchildren. These practices are sometimes described in terms of 'intergenerational reciprocity' (exchange of goods and services given to grandchildren for assistance provided by them to the grandmothers later in life; e.g. Apt 1996; van der Geest 1997b). We think that 'reciprocity'—implying exchanges between transacting agents—does not adequately describe these practices. Firstly, it focuses attention on material transactions among the many acts of sharing (time, pleasure, presence, touch, etc.). Considering Maria and Susanna's emphasis on 'love' as constituted by immaterial *and* material practices, one should instead see intimacy and consubstantiality as the dominant themes of sharing and transactions of objects or specific values, e.g. food or labour, as variations of these. Transactions of things are but the material pole of a continuum of sharing or relational practices. Secondly, the concept of exchange relies on individual subjects who transact in order to satisfy their needs, that is to retain or gain completeness. Sharing between grandmother and grandchild is instead rather about mutual complementation—mutual reliance is here not a means but the aim of social practice. Contrary to certain late modern Euro-American ideals of old age according to which autonomy should be maintained despite age, Maria's ideal of old age is being surrounded and cared for by her descendants. She is not assisted

---

and consumed, and which had no permanent inequalities in the distribution of the necessary things, as Luo society a few generations ago.

[15] Many traits of 'hunter–gatherer sharing' can be traced in Luo social practice. 'Demand sharing'—sharing instigated by a (legitimate) demand rather than generosity—resonates with Luo practices as described here; so does the observation that sharing includes material transfers among immaterial social gestures, and that sharing primarily makes persons, rather than solving distributional problems (Macdonald 2000). Bodenhorn's point (2000) that sharing, rather than reflecting essential kinship bonds, creates moments of satisfying unity that must be constantly renewed and that can create substantial relatedness, including bonds of kinship, as well as her analysis of sharing relations between humans and non-human beings, reveal parallels between Arctic hunters and Equatorial agriculturalists. These points cannot be followed up here, but invite further studies on the human propensity to share, drawing together new studies of relatedness and of economic relations.

by her grandchildren because she lost her own capacities; she has extended these through her grandchildren, sharing their hands and feet. This extension of one's capacity across others is not limited to bodily potentials: when Maria tells a story she often loses the thread or forgets details, and the grandchildren step in, filling gaps and reconstructing the plot. In this way they learn the narratives and, as their voices alternate and merge, they share in Maria's memories. Approaching death, Maria's capacities expand and embrace the children she lives with. This ability to let go, to extend into others until one vanishes is of course just another ideal, which is as difficult to live as that of autonomous ageing, and which does not exclude that one at times experiences and suffers from a loss of independence. Our point is that personal autonomy is only one possible frame to understand the practices between oldest and youngest and we cannot take it for granted, as notions of reciprocity and exchange implicitly do. Instead of economising human relations, regarding intergenerational transactions as potentially premised upon sharing would take seriously Maria's stress on 'love' or amity as the primary, though in practice difficult, social fact.

NEW WAYS, OLD TIES

Magdalene (b.1950)

To conclude, we turn to a third grandmother: Magdalene, Mercy's sister, and her classificatory granddaughter Jully (b.1997) who live in Kisumu city, a hundred kilometres from Uhero. Jully's mother Nell (b.1975), the daughter of Sister Mercy's husband's brother, was a single mother who had also taken in Jeremiah, the child of her restless younger sister, and lived with both Jully and Jeremiah in a rented room near Uhero. She called both Jeremiah and Jully 'my children', they called her 'mother', she slept with them in one bed and took care to treat them equally. However, when Nell began teacher training and had to move to a college, she sent Jully to a good, relatively expensive town school and left Jeremiah, whose maintenance she continued to pay, in the care of her younger brother in Uhero. She did this reluctantly and went to see Jeremiah as often as she could, but until she found other means, her priorities were for Jully, her own daughter. Although Nell did not wish to differentiate between own and classificatory children and tried to share her love, school fees forced a preference for the biological, 'own' child upon her.

Jully moved in with her grandmother Magdalene in Kisumu and with the three other children living there. Magdalene had no blood relation to Jully, but she had already lived with Nell (her sister's husband's brother's daughter) when the latter attended secondary school in Kisumu. For Nell, whose own mother and father were dead, she was a 'mother'. Taking Jully into her house and sharing her bed and table with her, Magdalene extended this school-fostering relation into the second, grandchild generation and nicknamed Jully accordingly 'my co-wife'. As she put it: 'This house here in O. [a modern housing estate in Kisumu] is now a *siwindhe*.' Here in the town, brought together by the requirements of schooling and based not on blood-bonds but affinal ties and shared daily lives, their tenderness and joking evoked that of old Maria and Susanna in the village. Magdalene expressed this continuity when she said (in English): 'We Luo grandmothers must sleep with our grandchildren, otherwise our beds are too cold. It is us who must take care of their development.' Yet Magdalene felt unable to take up Jeremiah together with Jully, as 'the house is too small', and 'we are not so closely related' (although genealogically he and Jully were equally unrelated to her). Nell's life with Magdalene had created a relation that, given limited space and means, distinguished the two grandchildren.

Sometimes Magdalene and Jully's quarrels differed from Maria and Susanna's; unlike most of her rural sisters, Jully did not usually yield when she was told to give, she wanted toys that could not be shared, and it happened that when someone referred to Magdalene as her 'grandmother' she blurted out 'This is not my grandmother', an explicit refusal of relatedness, which is considered rude even if one is not closely related. Going to a good school, learning English and Swahili, she acquired a sense of difference. When Jully quarrelled with her classificatory brother Dadi during a visit to her older grandmother Mercy in Uhero, Mercy jokingly commented: 'For her, he is now just a son of euphorbia (*ojuok*) [the traditional rural fence].' Magdalene occasionally complained about Jully's 'tough head', but their quarrels were embedded in the amity of their shared lives; moreover, being herself a single mother and hardworking employee at a department store, Magdalene acknowledged that 'girls, nowadays, need a hard head.' Most striking in their relation was the evident pleasure that Magdalene, returning from her 12-hour work-shifts, derived from a household that was teeming with children: 'If you are only two in the house and both of you are gloomy, there is silence. But if you are many, there is always somebody talking.'

This third grandmother and her child further blur the imagined dichotomy between Mercy's and Maria's lives as grandmothers. Within the urban life of this wage-earning grandmother and her well-groomed, ambitious granddaughter, practices of amity remain at the centre of everyday life and a source of pleasure and fulfilment. Schooling and school-knowledge do create distinctions and choices that enforce individual notions of person and property, but at the same time they provide opportunities for new relations, which engage seemingly older forms of sociality and everyday practice in new situations. Magdalene's life with Jully underlines, as do the tensions and dilemma's in Maria's and Mercy's lives, that these grandmothers are modern subjects, split between different options of fashioning themselves and imagining others and between different modes of practising relatedness, and forced to situate themselves on a fragmented terrain.

CONCLUSION

In this paper we examined some aspects of the relationship between grandmothers and grandchildren, an important axis in the lives of most *JoUhero*. The practices of address and sharing are important in this relationship and for the production of sociality in general, and in both areas of practice, different ways of being and becoming a person, and different modes of engaging with the boundaries between self and other are enacted. A name can be owned as a marker of unequivocal personal identity or used as a fluid practice of nearness, which brings one in touch with others in changeable, ambiguous and inclusive ways. Playful giving and taking of objects introduces transactions as a mode of being towards the other *before* one's subjectivity and possessions are conceived. We suggested that sharing is thereby introduced as a practice that is different from exchange and reciprocity, and that is central to Uhero sociality. The differences and tensions between practices of personhood that emphasise the individual subject and agent, and those that emphasise relatedness as the source of subjectivity, and the bond with the other before the self, are more visible and explicit in some areas of everyday life and discourse than in others. Schooling—a key area of modern advancement and 'strategic' practice in de Certeau's sense (1984: 34)—is a field in which the contrasts are more evident. In more diffuse practices like play with children, these contrasts work implicitly.

As the stories of Maria and Susanna, Mercy and Dadi, and Magdalene and Jully show, life in Uhero rarely affords fixed positions in this dichotomous framework: children have proper names and nicknames; people must aim to accumulate to attain their ends, but most continue to share; children should go to school, and the property-nature of the school's ideology of knowledge forces everybody into compromises. Despite the societal changes that have transformed the lives and relations of people in Uhero between the time of the grandmothers and that of the grandchildren, their relations embody fundamental values and valued social practices. Irrespective of the different lives of the three grandmothers described here, their everyday continues to centre around their relations with grandchildren and the pleasure they derive from the tenderness and closeness between them, which all three of them call 'love'.

ACKNOWLEDGEMENTS

We are grateful to 'Sister Mercy' and her late husband, to 'Maria' and 'Magdalene', and to their families, for their hospitality and patience, which we hope they will extend to the shortcomings of this account. Thanks to Philister Adhiambo Madiega and Emmah Odundo who worked with us! We thank the participants of our ASA panel and Susan Benson for their comments. Our research is supported by the Council for Development Research of the Danish International Development Agency, the Institute of Anthropology at the University of Copenhagen, the Danish Bilharziasis Laboratory, the Kenyan–Danish Health Research Project, the Wenner-Gren Foundation, the Research Project on Ageing at the University of Copenhagen and the Smuts and the Rivers Funds, University of Cambridge.

REFERENCES

Abe, T. 1981. 'The concepts of Chira and Dhoch among the Luo of Kenya: transition, deviation and misfortune', in N. Nagashima (ed.), *Themes in*

Socio-Cultural Ideas and Behaviour among the Six Ethnic Groups of Kenya: the Visukha, the Iteso, the Gusii, the Kipsigis, the Luo, and the Kamba. Kinutachi, Tokyo: Hitotsubashi University.

Apt, N. A. 1996. *Coping with Old Age in a Changing Africa: social change and the elderly Ghanaian.* Aldershot: Avebury.

Blacking, J. 1990. 'Growing old gracefully: physical, social and spiritual transformations in Venda society, 1956–66', in P. Spencer (ed.), *Anthropology and the Riddle of the Sphinx: paradoxes of change in the life course.* London: Routledge.

Blount, B. G. 1971. 'Aspects of Luo Socialization'. Institute of African Studies Discussion Paper No. 23. Nairobi: Institute of African Studies, University of Nairobi.

Bodenhorn, B. 2000. 'It is good to know who your relatives are but we are taught to share with everybody: shares and sharing among Inupiaq households', in G. W. Wenzel, G. Hovelsrud-Broda, and N. Kishigami (eds), *The Social Economy of Sharing: resource allocation and modern hunter–gatherers.* Osaka: National Museum of Ethnology.

Brindley, M. 1986a. 'The role of old women in Zulu culture: old women and child-nurture', *South African Journal of Ethnology* 9 (1): 26–31.

——1986b. 'The role of old women in Zulu culture: the old woman and adolescence', *South African Journal of Ethnology* 9 (3): 120–128.

Cattell, M. G. 1992. 'Praise the Lord and say no to men: older women empowering themselves in Samia, Kenya', *Journal of Cross-Cultural Gerontology* 7: 307–30.

de Certeau, M. 1984. *The Practice of Everyday Life.* Trans. by Steven Rendall. Berkley: University of California Press. (1980. *L'Invention du quotidien. 1. Arts de Faire.* Paris: Union Générale d'Editions.)

Cohen, D. W. 1985. 'Doing social history from Pim's doorway', in O. Zunz (ed.), *Reliving the Past: the worlds of social history.* Chapel Hill NC and London: University of North Carolina Press.

Cohen, D. W., and E. S. A. Odhiambo. 1989. *Siaya: the historical anthropology of an African landscape.* Nairobi: Heineman Kenya.

Erny, P. 1981. *The Child and his Environment in Black Africa.* Revised translation by G. J. Wanjohi. Nairobi and New York: Oxford University Press. (1972. *L'Enfant et son milieu en Afrique noire. Essais sur l'éducation traditionelle.* Paris: Payot.)

Evans-Pritchard, E. E. 1965. 'Marriage customs of the Luo of Kenya', in E. E. Evans-Pritchard, *The Position of Women in Primitive Societies and Other Essays in Social Anthropology.* London: Faber & Faber.

Fortes, M. 1938. 'Social and psychological aspects of education in Taleland', *Africa* 11 (Supplement) (4): 1–64.

——1949. *The Web of Kinship among the Tallensi: the second part of an analysis of the social structure of a Trans-Volta tribe.* London: Oxford University Press, for the International African Institute.

Geissler, P. W., S. A. Harris, R. J. Prince, A. Olsen, R. Achieng' Odhiambo, H. Oketch-Rabah, A. Andersen, and P. Mølgaard. 2002. 'Medicinal plants used by Luo mothers and children in Bondo District, Kenya', *Journal of Ethnopharmacology,* in press.

Grigorenko, E. L., P. W. Geissler, R. J. Prince, F. Okatcha, K. Nokes, D. A. Kenny, D. A. Bundy, and R. J. Sternberg. 1999. 'The organisation of Luo conceptions of intelligence: a study of implicit theories in a Kenyan village', *Journal of Behavioural Development* 25 (4): 367–378.

Hauge, H.-E. 1974. *Luo Religion and Folklore.* Oslo, Bergen and Tromsø: Universitetsforlaget.

Heald, S. 1999. 'Joking and avoidance, hostility and incest: an essay on Gisu moral categories', in S. Heald (ed.), *Manhood and Morality: sex, violence, and ritual in Gisu society*. London and New York: Routledge.

Holmes, E. R., and L. D. Holmes. 1995. *Other Cultures, Elder Years*. Second edition. Thousand Oaks CA and London: Sage Publications.

Holy, L. 1990. 'Strategies for the old age among the Berti of the Sudan', in P. Spencer (ed.), *Anthropology and the Riddle of the Sphinx: paradoxes of change in the life course*. London: Routledge.

Hunt, R. C. 2000. 'Forager food sharing economy: transfers and exchanges', in G. W. Wenzel, G. Hovelsrud-Broda, and N. Kishigami (eds), *The Social Economy of Sharing: resource allocation and modern hunter–gatherers*. Osaka: National Museum of Ethnology.

James, W. 1978. 'Matrifocus on African women', in S. Ardener (ed.), *Defining Females: the nature of women in society*. New York: Wiley.

Kidd, D. 1906. *Savage Childhood: a study of Kafir children*. London: Adam & Charles Black.

Lancy, D. F. 1996. *Playing on the Mother-ground: cultural routines for children's development*. New York and London: Guilford Press.

Lévinas, E. 1985. 'Vom Bewußtsein zur Wachheit', in E. Lévinas, *Wenn Gott ins Denken einfällt. Diskurse über die Betroffenheit von Transzendenz*. Freiburg and München: Alber. (1982. 'De la conscience à la veille', in E. Lévinas, *De Dieu qui vient à l'idée*. Paris: J. Vrin.)

Lienhardt, G. 1985. 'Self: public, private. Some African representations', in M. Carrithers, S. Collins, and S. Lukes (eds), *The Category of the Person: anthropology, philosophy, history*. Cambridge: Cambridge University Press.

Macdonald, G. 2000. 'Economies and personhood: demand sharing among the Wiradjuri of New South Wales', in G. W. Wenzel, G. Hovelsrud-Broda, and N. Kishigami (eds), *The Social Economy of Sharing: resource allocation and modern hunter–gatherers*. Osaka: National Museum of Ethnology.

MacGoye, M. O. 1993. *Victoria. Murder in Majengo*. London and Basingstoke: Macmillan.

Mboya, P. 1983. (1938). *Luo: Kitgi gi Timbegi. A hanbook of Luo customs*. Kisumu: Anyange Press.

Mead, M. 1967. 'Ethnological aspects of aging', *Psychosomatics* 8: 33–37.

Nyambedha, E. O. 2000. 'Support Systems for Orphaned Children in Nyangoma Sub-location, Bondo District, Western Kenya'. M.Sc. thesis. Nairobi: Institute of African Studies, University of Nairobi.

Ocholla-Ayayo, A. B. C. 1976. *Traditional Ideology and Ethics among the Southern Luo*. Uppsala: Scandinavian Institute of African Studies.

Odinga, O. 1967. *Not yet Uhuru: the autobiography of Oginga Odinga*. London, Ibadan and Nairobi: Heinemann Educational Books.

Ogola, M. A. 1994. *The River and the Source*. Nairobi: Focus Books.

Ogot, P. (Pamela Kola). 1966. *East African How? Stories*. East African Junior Library, no. 2. Nairobi: East African Publishing House.

Ominde, S. H. 1952. *The Luo Girl from Infancy to Marriage*. Nairobi: East African Literature Bureau.

Onyango-Ogutu, B., and A. A. Roscoe. 1974. *Keep My Words*. Nairobi: East African Publishing House.

Otiende, J. E., S. P. Wamahiu, and A. M. Karugu. 1992. *Education and Development in Kenya: a historical perspective*. Nairobi: Oxford University Press.

Parkin, D. J. 1978. *The Cultural Definition of Political Response: lineal destiny among the Luo*. London and New York: Academic Press.

Potash, B. 1978. 'Some aspects of marital stability in a rural Luo community', *Africa* 48 (4): 380–397.

——1986. 'Wives of the graves: widows in a rural Luo community', in B. Potash (ed.), *Widows in African Societies: choices and constraints*. Stanford CA: Stanford University Press.

Prince, R. J., and P. W. Geissler. 2001. 'Becoming "One who treats": a case study of a Luo healer and her grandson in western Kenya', *Anthropology & Education Quarterly* 32(4): 447–471.

Prince, R.J., P. W. Geissler, K. Nokes, F. Okatcha, E. L. Grigorenko, and R. J. Sternberg. 2001. 'Knowledge of herbal and pharmaceutical medicines among Luo schoolchildren in western Kenya', *Anthropology and Medicine* 8 (2/3): 211–237.

Prince, R. J., P. W. Geissler, G. Tuchtenhagen, and M. Neubert-Maric. 2002. *Adhiambo—born in the evening. Two months in the life of a Kenyan mother and her newborn daughter*. Digital video film, 68 mins. Hamburg, Copenhagen and Cambridge: Royal Anthropological Institute.

Radcliffe-Brown, A. R. 1940. 'On joking relationships', *Africa* 13 (3): 195–210. Reprinted 1979 in A. R. Radcliffe-Brown, *Structure and Function in Primitive Societies: essays and addresses*. London and Henley: Routledge & Kegan Paul.

——1949. 'A further note on joking relationships', *Africa* 19 (2): 133–140. Reprinted 1979 in A. R. Radcliffe-Brown, *Structure and Function in Primitive Societies: essays and addresses*. London and Henley: Routledge & Kegan Paul.

Raum, O. F. 1940. *Chaga Childhood: a description of indigenous education in an East African tribe*. London: Oxford University Press, for the International Institute of African Languages and Cultures.

Reynolds, P. 1986. 'The training of traditional healers in Mashonaland', in M. Last and G. L. Chavunduka (eds), *The Professionalisation of African Medicine*. Manchester: Manchester University Press, for the International African Institute.

——1996. *Traditional Healers and Childhood in Zimbabwe*. Athens: Ohio University Press.

Serpell, R. 1993. *The Significance of Schooling: life-journeys in an African society*. Cambridge and New York: Cambridge University Press.

Taylor, C. C. 1992. *Milk, Honey and Money: changing concepts in Rwandan healing*. Washington DC and London: Smithsonian Institution Press.

Turner, V. 1955. 'The spatial separation of adjacent genealogical generations in Ndembu village structure', *Africa* 25: 121–137.

——1996. *Schism and Continuity in an African Society: a study of Ndembu village life*. Oxford: Berg.

Van der Geest, S. 1997a. 'Between respect and reciprocity: managing old age in rural Ghana', *Southern African Journal of Gerontology* 6 (2): 20–25.

——1997b. 'Money and respect: the changing value of old age in rural Ghana', *Africa* 67 (4): 534–559.

Waligorski, A. 1968. 'Kinship terminology of the Luo', *Africana Bulletin* 8: 57–63.

Wenzel, G. W., G. Hovelsrud-Broda, and N. Kishigami (eds). 2000. *The Social Economy of Sharing: resource allocation and modern hunter–gatherers*. Osaka: National Museum of Ethnology.

Whyte, S. R. 1990. 'The widow's dream: sex and death in western Kenya', in M. Jackson and I. Karp (eds), *Personhood and Agency: the experience of self and other in African cultures*. Acta Universitatis Upsaliensis, 14. Uppsala: S. Academiae Ubsaliensis.

——1997. *Questioning Misfortune: the pragmatics of uncertainty in Eastern Uganda*. Cambridge: Cambridge University Press.

Woodburn, J. 1998. ' "Sharing is not a form of exchange": an analysis of property sharing in immediate-return hunter–gatherer societies', in C. M. Hann (ed.), *Property Relations: renewing the anthropological tradition*. Cambridge: Cambridge University Press.

ABSTRACT

This essay explores the relationships between three Luo grandmothers and their grandchildren with particular attention to forms of address and of sharing as practices of amity. Classic Africanist kinship studies identified these as central to the relations between alternate generations. We argue that they are also crucial to our understanding of some aspects of the notion of 'love' (*hera*) that old and young Luo describe as constitutive both of grandmotherhood in particular and of sociality in general. We shall intertwine these concerns of the first generation of social anthropologists, in what were then imagined as pre-modern societies, with the concerns that contemporary, modern Luo grandmothers and grandchildren have with love. Love or amity, and their attendant everyday practices of sharing, retain their importance both for the grandmaternal bond and for broader Luo sociality. Rather than providing an unquestioned and unequivocal prescriptive framework, these practices of relatedness are situated within an imaginative field which is often explicitly dichotomised. Some practices stress individual selves and autonomous subjects, while others emphasise the sharedness of the self and the primacy of relations over subjects. Rather than adhering to one or the other of these poles of relatedness and personhood, modern Luo grandmothers and grandchildren create their everyday lives between them, drawing on divergent ideas and practices, while enjoying, where possible, the pleasures of 'love'.

RÉSUMÉ

Cet essai examine les relations entre trois grands-mères luos et leurs petits-enfants, et plus particulièrement les formes d'adresse et de partage en tant que pratiques d'amitié. Les études africanistes classiques sur la parenté les ont identifiées comme étant au cœur des relations entre générations alternes. L'article montre qu'elles sont également essentielles pour comprendre certains aspects de la notion d'«amour» (*hera*) que les vieux et jeunes Luo décrivent comme constitutifs de la sociabilité en général et de la grand-maternité en particulier. Il mêle ces préoccupations de la première génération d'anthropologues sociaux, dans ce que l'on imaginait alors être des sociétés pré-modernes, avec les préoccupations des grands-mères et petits-enfants modernes et contemporains concernant l'amour. L'amour et l'amitié, et les pratiques quotidiennes de partage qui leur sont associées, conservent leur importance pour le lien grand-maternel et plus largement pour la sociabilité luo. Plutôt que de fournir un cadre prescriptif incontesté et sans équivoque, ces pratiques de parenté se situent dans un champ imaginatif souvent explicitement dichotomisé. Certaines pratiques mettent l'accent sur le moi individuel et le sujet autonome, tandis que d'autres soulignent la qualité de partage du moi et la primauté de la relation sur le sujet. Plutôt que d'adhérer à l'un ou l'autre de ces pôles de parenté et d'individualité, les grands-mères et petits-enfants luos modernes bâtissent leur existence quotidienne entre les deux, usant d'idées et de pratiques divergentes tout en jouissant, lorsque c'est possible, des plaisirs de l'«amour».